Homeless People Are Human Beings Too

Homeless People Are Human Beings Too

Leo Gnawa

Self-Published ~By~ Leo Gnawa

Copyright ©2024 Leo Gnawa

All rights reserved

No part of this book may be reproduced, stored in a retrieval system, or transmitted in any form, of by any means, electronic, mechanical, photocopying, recording or otherwise. Without prior permission of the publisher.

First Edition

ISBN: 9798324115043

.

I dedicate it to all the children who are homeless.

TABLE OF CONTENTS:

Chapter 1: The Raccoon Who Stole The Homeless Man Oatmeal Cream Pies: ---Page 1

Chapter 2: The Dead Deer By My Tent ---Page 5

Chapter 3: The Kids Who Laughed At A Homeless Man ---Page 7

Chapter 4: A Hole In The Roof Above My Bed ---Page 11

Chapter 5: Underpaying And Overworking Homeless Workers ---Page 15

Chapter 6: The Moving Company Paid Homeless Men Less Than They Worked For ---Page 17

Chapter 7: Attacked On The Bus By A Young Man--Page 21

Chapter 8: An Eviction Notice To A Homeless Man Living Outside ----Page 25

Chapter 9: The Police Officer Falsely Accusing Homeless Man Of Breaking Into A Car --- Page 29

Chapter 10: Kicking The Homeless Outside In The Cold --- Page 35

Chapter 11: The Homeless Woman Who Waited In Vain For The Shelter Van --- Page 39

Chapter 12: Homeless Man Who Had A Place But Was Sleeping Outside ---Page 43

Chapter 13: Restaurant Security Not Letting Me Use Restrooms Because I Look Homeless ---Page 47

Chapter 14: I Got Diagnosed With Type Two Diabetes ---Page 51

Chapter 15: The Mc Donald Cashier Who Refused To Sell Coffee To A Homeless Man ---Page 55

Chapter 16: They Set The Food On The Floor, I Refused It. ---Page 69

Chapter 17: The Kids Who Gave Me A $1 For My Book ---Page 75

Chapter 18: Who am I? I am Not Happy ---Page 81

Chapter 19: A Homeless Man Survival In The Woods Through The Corona Virus Pandemic ---Page 85

Chapter 20: Words Of Inspiration ---Page 105

Chapter 21: Homelessness Is Not A Choice ---Page 113

Chapter 22: Message From A Homeless Man To Young People ---Page 121

Conclusion: Myths & Facts About Homelessness ---Page 121

Why Do People Experience Homelessness? --- Page 135

INTRODUCTION:

I have been selling my books on the streets in Washington DC for years, as a self-published author who experienced chronic homelessness. A chronic homeless is a person who has experienced homelessness off and on for a long time. I was homeless when I wrote my first book and started selling it on the streets in downtown Washington DC. Now, I have been able to keep a roof over my head, by selling my books and saving whatever I could, in order to afford and pay for a place to live.

Many times, my best customers have been children and teenagers walking by me with their parents and asking them to buy one of my books for them.

The parents on many occasions asked me which of my books would be good for their children. Sometimes, the kids would just grab a book that they wanted. I was happy to see kids and young folks being interested in buying my books to read or just support me. But I have always been concerned that some of the content in the books may be too traumatic and too adult for children and young folks.

This book is therefore a PG 13-like version of my story for young folks. In this book you still have many of the stories that are in my other books. Their purpose is to create awareness about homelessness through my experience with homelessness.

I want young people to have compassion and empathy for the homeless and not be mean to them. I have seen young people make fun of homeless people, including myself. I have a story in the book about it.

I have seen young people be violent towards homeless people, including myself. In my 3 previous books, I have shared some of my personal experience as well as the experience of other homeless people, included myself, being attacked and harmed by young folks. I only shared one of the stories in this book because they are too traumatic.

I want young people to be aware that although we are of different races, religions, ideologies, political affiliations, gender, social status, all of us are one and the same human species. We have the same blood color, same humanity, same desire for peace, health, happiness, and prosperity.

Everything that causes other human beings to experience unhappiness and suffering, particularly issues regarding poverty, human dignity, human rights, and the environment should concern all of us, including young people. They are the future generations who may end homelessness.

CHAPTER I

THE RACCOON WHO STOLE THE HOMELESS MAN OATMEAL CREAM PIES:

One night, a raccoon stole a homeless man oatmeal cream pies, while he was asleep in his tent.

He had finished selling copies of his book on a street corner half-a-block away from the White House, where the President of the United States resides and works.

He was a 50-year-old homeless who decided to write a book and self-publish it. His goal was to use his writings to create awareness about homelessness. He also wanted to sell them to make enough money to afford a place to call home and not live outside in a tent anymore.

Writing a book was not easy, and selling it was even harder. But he was proud to have become a self-published homeless author who was willing to go sell copies of his book outside. He enjoyed waking up every day and going to sell his book on the street corner, to earn some money to take care of himself, and to hopefully save enough to get himself out of homelessness.

Living in a tent in the bushes alone was scary, but he was not afraid. The area was peaceful enough, despite the noise of insects and birds in the trees and grasses around his tent.

One day, he came back to the tent at night and found a dead dear by a tree close to the tent. Another time, he saw a Cayote lurking around when he was eating some fish that he brought with him. And one time, he stepped on a fox sleeping in the bushes not far from his tent. But, he never was attacked by any animal.

There were a highway and few exit roads linked to an overpass bridge, around the area where he set up his tent under a pine tree.

One night, at around 11 pm, he stopped at a 24-hour Safeway grocery store on New York Avenue and 4th Street in North West Washington DC to grab whatever he needed to fix himself a meal later. He had just finished selling his books downtown and was heading back to his tent. He had some tuna cans in his tent. He bought some potato salad and some bread or crackers to eat with the tuna. He also got a box of Little Debbie's oatmeal pies, a bottle of juice of either grapefruit, apple or pineapple, or some lemonade.

He got into his tent, made a quick tuna sandwich meal, ate it voraciously and went to sleep right away, because he was totally exhausted. He awoke in the middle of his sleep, opened the box of Oatmeal Pies, pulled out a couple of the pies and munched on them while half asleep.

THE RACCOON WHO STOLE THE HOMELESS MAN OATMEAL PIES

A couple of hours later, almost around 4am, He tried to grab a couple more pies out of the box, while he had his eyes closed and was not fully awaken. He patted around the bed in his tent but could not feel the box. He sat up and used a flashlight to look all over the bed since it was pitch dark in the tent, but the box was not there. He guessed that he might have knocked the oatmeal cream pies box out the bed accidentally while asleep. He directed the flashlight towards the bottom side of the bed. Guess what he saw? You won't believe it. Some bright eyes were shining in the darkness by a box of copies of his book in the bottom right corner of the tent. A raccoon was enjoying an early breakfast on the homeless man Little Debbie's oatmeal cream pies.

The homeless man run out of that tent like a scared little boy. He realized that he had a serious problem and needed to get rid it of it right away. At times, field mice managed to get inside the tent by chewing holes into the tent canvas' walls. The raccoon most likely got inside the tent through one of the holes. The homeless man worst nightmare was to come home one day and find a raccoon, a snake, and a possum inside the tent. But it never happened until then. Mosquitoes, flies, and ants were frequent uninvited guests, but a raccoon in the tent was out of question. It had to go one way or another.

The homeless man feared that getting bitten by the raccoon could get him infected with rabies. Rabies is a deadly virus transmitted to a person from the saliva of an infected animal through a bite. Raccoons have the reputation of carrying rabies

Sorry, Mister Raccoon had to go. The homeless man kept a metal pole in the tent for protection. He grabbed it, stepped outside, and smacked on the outside of the tent to scare the raccoon and force it to come out, without hurting it. But Mister Raccoon had no intention of exiting that tent. It kept moving from one corner of the tent to another. The homeless man grabbed the mattress, pulled it out, did the same with the mattress box and turned the tent around. The Raccoon found itself outside, strolled towards a small tree, climbed it and stayed on a branch.

The homeless man found the hole in the tent and patched it, then went about his day away from the area to get on the shower list, at a place that was providing day services to the homeless.

He spent the night outside working on his laptop. He used an outside electric outlet to fully charge it. He returned early in the morning around 6:00 am, peeped in the small tree and did not see the raccoon. Guess who was in there when he unzipped the door of his tent. The raccoon was chilling in a plastic basket inside the entrance of the tent. The homeless man was sleepy and did not need company. So, he got the raccoon out and chased it all the way to the bridge, by the spot where he kept his trash. He felt like the raccoon would be pleased to check out the trash and happy to find some leftover food in there. The homeless man was me.

CHAPTER 2

THE DEAD DEER BY MY TENT

I was walking to my tent on the partly snow-covered grass when I saw something shaped like an animal lying down next to a tree fifty feet from my tent.

My poor eyesight made it hard for me to see clearly in the darkness of the night, what it was and whether it was alive or dead. I was a bit worried and wondered that it could be a wounded wolf resting under the tree. I grabbed a metal pole and tiptoed carefully towards the thing until I could clearly see that it was a deer on the snow.

I walked back to my tent, got some sheets of towel paper, walked back to the dead deer, grabbed its leg, and dragged it close to the road, so that drivers see it in the morning and call the authorities to remove it.

I left early in the morning and went to the downtown area of the city to shower at the day center for the homeless and take care of other needs. I returned to my tent in the bushes in the evening and was surprised to see the dead animal still there. I went inside my tent and slept. I was a bit anxious but relieved that the ground was covered with snow and the temperature slightly above freezing. That meant that deer's corpse would not deteriorate fast enough to attract predators and vultures.

I was up early in the morning but waited until 10:00am to call the city's animal removal service. A lady answered and told me that she already received several calls and that a team was on the way to remove the dead deer. I was glad to hear that and left for the day.

Guess what happened when I came back that night? The dead dear was still there. I knew what to do for an emergency crew to be urgently dispatched to remove the carcass. I dragged and left it close enough to the road's surface, at the intersection where the exit road merges into the main road. Any driver would see the dead deer when they turn into the highway.

I do not know if the city animal removal service removed it, or if a driver picked it up and put it in his trunk to take it home and turn it into a meal. But I was relieved that the dead deer was gone, and I returned to my tent the fourth night.

CHAPTER 3

THE KIDS WHO LAUGHED AT A HOMELESS MAN

He had left his tent in the woods and was on his way to a soup kitchen known as SOME. It is the acronym for So Other People Can Eat. It was a well-known soup Kitchen in Washington DC, where homeless folks and poor men, women from different parts of the city, used to go there, sometimes with their children, to have breakfast and lunch. He had lunch there and headed to a nearby small library located near a low-income housing project called Sumsum Corda.

He was walking behind a man who looked like he was homeless also. Both of them were walking to the Northwest One Library. They were passing the fence of the Terrel Recreational Center contiguous to the library, when the one behind saw a group of school kids throw rocks from the playground, at the homeless in front of him. Most of them were girls around the ages of 9 to 11 or even younger. He kept his eyes on them because he was anticipating that they would also throw rocks at him, as soon as his back was turned towards them.

They stood there with rocks in their hands and proceeded towards the fence, like a pack of wolves advancing towards their prey, as he made it towards the middle of the outside of the fence.

"Hey, you boy, I will punch you in the face, boy" a couple of them yelled at the 50-year-old homeless man. He was shocked to hear these kids behave so disrespectfully towards a man old enough to be their grandfather.

"I'm old enough to be your father. You have to respect people old enough to be your parents" he hollered at them.

Another little girl noticed the navy back pack he was carrying and his not-so-well-kept appearance. She shouted he homeless". The rest joined in and started screaming "He homeless, he homeless". It seemed like they were having fun making fun of this older person because he was homeless.

The homeless man was baffled and felt bad, sad, and humiliated. He wondered whether he would have felt as hurt as he was if they had thrown rocks at him instead of mocking him. The irony is that these kids or some of them, probably resided in or around the Sumsum Corda neighborhood and in the housing complexes in the vicinity. Majority of the residents were poor people housed there through government assistance and vouchers programs. That meant that the parents of many of them were also poor people who might have experienced homelessness in their past.

"You may end up becoming homeless yourself. You never know," he told the most aggressive of them. She held her hips with both hands and retorted "I will never be homeless", while wiggling from side to side and leaning her torso forward.

The homeless man responded "How you know that? Don't laugh at homeless people. Pray that you do not become homeless when you grow up." He was surprised that no adult was out there to watch over these kids on the playground. But he heard one of them say, "We are not supposed to talk to strangers".

The homeless man felt relieved when he reached the end of the fence safely, after the hurtful conversation he initiated, successfully distracted and deterred them from throwing rocks at him. Nonetheless, he was still hurt by them mocking him for being homeless. The homeless man was me.

If these kids had considered for one second that they and their parents could become homeless in the future, I am certain that they would have expressed empathy instead of making fun of me or any person experiencing homelessness.

Never put down or make fun of anybody because they are too poor to afford a place to live, food to eat or even nice clothes and shoes like you. What happened to them could happen to anybody else or to someone related or acquainted to you.

Consider yourself fortunate if you never experienced poverty and never been in a situation when you or your parents were unable to take care of your basic needs. Be grateful that you have a good life and everything you need.

CHAPTER 4:

A HOLE IN THE ROOF ABOVE MY BED

I was renting a room at a rooming house on the corner of Rhode Island Avenue and 3rd Street in Northwest Washington DC. The place was a mess and not suitable for human habitation. The building was decayed and infested with rodents. I could hear rats or mice squeaking and moving around in my room, in the hallway and in the kitchen, when I was in my bed at night and the lights were turned off.

One day, as soon as I opened the front door of the building downstairs, a rat sprang from outside into the staircase and sprinted upstairs in front of me. I came home another day and turned on the light, but there was no electricity in the building. I walked upstairs in the dark and was informed by the guy who occupied the first room by the stairs that, there had been an electric fire in the building earlier. The firemen had punched a hole in the roof above my room in order to get to the top of the building through the roof right above my bed. The door was wide open when I walked in. I found debris scattered everywhere and all over the bed. I could see the sky through the huge hole above my bed. Nobody cared to clean the mess in the room or cover the hole in the roof. I had to go outside to find some plywood and cardboards and cover the hole myself.

Yet, the landlord, slumlord shall I say, collected the rent every Friday, during the whole month that we were deprived of electricity. The hole in my roof was not fixed until I moved to the room next door a month later, after it was vacated by the previous renter. He knew that it was not easy to find rooms as cheap as his, in the city. Besides, he felt like, we were homeless and fortunate to have him rent us rooms, although we had no reliable sources of income besides working on day jobs. I had no money to pay the rent sometimes, when day labor became scarce in the winter.

When I came home one Friday night, my door had padlock on it. I was a week late on my rent. I had to wait until the morning to see the landlord to get inside my room. He run a nasty rat-infested restaurant located at the bottom of the building. I used to ask myself, who were those customers crazy enough to come and eat there. I decided to just leave that night. I never returned. I had no money to pay him. I was also tired of living in a filthy place. On top of that, I was being pressured to pay rent for a week that I was late, while I paid rent for a whole month for a room without electricity and with a hole in the roof. Whatever happened to my belongings is anybody guess. I was back on the streets as homeless again and lost all my belongings.

CHAPTER 5

UNDERPAYING OVERWORKED HOMELESS LABOR WORKERS

Like many other homeless staying at the CCNV shelter, I was waiting at the corner of 2nd Street and D Street to hop on any van or truck pulling up there to take folks to go to work on day jobs. Many of us used to get up at 5 am to have a better chance to be picked before it got crowded with more folks trying to go to work. Day labor sub-contractors and agencies targeted homeless men and women to work for them for less money than the jobs were worth.

Folks who argue that people are homeless because they are lazy and do not want to work are not right. There might be some homeless who do not want to work. But many folks who are fully employed are homeless because they do not earn enough to pay rent.

"Leo, my man about to pull up" said to me another homeless man who was a friend. The sub-contractor that he worked for daily, had asked him to gather a crew of 5 hard working homeless men. "What y'all be doin'" I asked him. "We be moving store and kitchen equipment" he responded. "It is some hard work. You wanna go?" He asked me. "No problem. How much he pay?" I asked. "$40 for the day" was his answer. Few minutes later, a pickup truck pulled up and we all got on it. I was the only one new on the truck. The others were regulars. The boss let me get on the truck and asked me if I could handle hard work. I responded yes. We were six homeless laborers in total.

He drove to somewhere in Maryland where we picked a commercial restaurant range, loaded it on the truck and unloaded it at a restaurant kitchen. I never lifted anything so heavy in my entire life. We picked up more store and restaurant equipment and dropped them at several locations in Maryland and Washington DC. We worked all day for no less than 8 hours straight hours. The man asked me if I was willing to come back to work for him the next day. He was pleased with my work and wanted to keep me as one of his regulars. He paid me $50 and gave the others $40.

I promised him that I would be ready in the morning. But honestly speaking, lifting 600 and plus pound of heavy metal equipment for $40 or $50 was not worth it. I was desperate for the money but was not too sure if I wanted to do this again. I could barely get up when I woke up at 5am the next day. My entire body was sore. I decided not to go back because I was in pain and unwilling to go kill myself for 8 hours for only $50. I did not go.

CHAPTER 6

THE MOVING COMPANY PAID HOMELESS MEN LESS THAN THEY WORKED FOR

I stood outside the CCNV homeless shelter where I was staying and jumped in the back of a moving company truck, when its owner pulled up to pick up homeless men who were waited outside to go to do any labor work. The owner of the company asked me if I had done moving jobs before. All the guys who got on the truck had worked for him before. I was a new face on the truck. I told him that I never did. He let me stay on. I ended up enjoying the job. I was outside ready to go to work with him, anytime he showed up at the shelter. I still liked the job although he did not pay us much, compared to the work we put in. We were getting tips from most of his customers, but he kept it when the tips were added the amount that he was billing them for the job, unless the customers handed it to us separately and directly. Some of the homeless workers waited until they were alone with the customers and told them that if they were going to tip us, they should give us the tips, because he would keep it to himself if they gave it to him for us.

On many occasions, a couple of the guys and I were sent alone with one his truck to do move some of his customers from one state to another. He used a couple of the homeless guys as drivers to go on some of the jobs when he had multiple moving jobs at the same time. We made good money from the tips we were getting on these moving assignments.

Most of the other guys were nonchalant on the jobs mostly when we were alone on the job and the boss was not with us. I always stood out as one of the hardest working man on any crew I was on whether in the presence or absence of the boss. On one of the job, the client approached me approached me while I was away from the other workers. He made the remark that I was working harder than the rest of the crew. He expressed his appreciation from my hard work, handed me a $100 tip and advised me to think about starting my own moving company in the future. I am not sure if he tipped the other workers. If he did, it was nothing near what he gave me. We were paid $100 for the job. I made twice what I was paid for. Packing and loading a whole house on a truck and traveling to another state and unloading and unpacking everything was worth more than $100 for the 24 hour and plus we spent on the job. But as homeless men, we did any job, to make money to afford better food than what was served at the shelter and also to take care of basic needs.

One Saturday, after we finished working, the boss assigned me and another worker to a moving job in Virginia for the next morning. He has something else to do and did not plan to go with us. He gave us transportation money for us to get on the metro train. We were both staying at the shelter.

I got up early that Sunday morning, took a shower and went and got on the train on my way to the job. I thought the other guy was also on his way there since we did not leave together. But he was not there when I arrived at the location near the subway station in Alexandria, Virginia. I called the boss. He was in Baltimore, Maryland.

The other guy did not have a phone, nor did I. But I used a pay phone at the metro station to call the boss and told him that I got there by myself and have not seen the other guy. He told me to go ahead and do the job by myself and collect the $500 check from the customer and give it to him, the next day when he comes to pick us up at the shelter in the morning to go to work.

The customers, a couple, were waiting by the van outside. The job consisted of unloading the van containing all their belongings, mostly furniture, from their previous residence and taking everything upstairs to their new apartment. They probably hired a moving company from the state they move from, to move their stuff to the van and drove the van to their new location. They had requested and were being billed for two workers. They wondered why I was alone. They were not sure whether I could do the job alone. I explained to them that another guy was supposed to come with me, but I was not certain whether he was going to show up or not. I told them not to worry and assured them that I could do the job alone.

I went ahead and unloaded all the furniture and everything else off the truck, loaded them on the apartment complex's freight elevator, unloaded them upstairs and carried everything to the apartment piece by piece.

The customers, a husband, and his wife, were pleased with the work I did. But they were very upset to see me doing all the work by myself, although they were being billed for two workers. The wife asked me how much I was going to be paid for the job. I told her $40 dollars. Both were in disbelief. The wife told her husband to write the $500 check to me instead of writing it to the moving company boss. I explained to her that I was a homeless guy staying at the shelter, and that I relied on the job with the moving company boss to earn money daily like the other homeless workers of his. I could not jeopardize that job by keeping the $500 for myself. The couple decided to write a $300 check in the moving company's boss name and give me $200 in cash for myself. They thought that it was not fair for him to make all that money while I did all the job alone.

CHAPTER 7:

THE YOUNG MAN WHO ATTACKED ME ON THE BUS:

I got on the number 80 bus on 12th and H street, at about 9 pm, on my way to my tent in the bushes, after I was done selling my books downtown. It was normally a 10 minutes bus ride. I went to sit all the way in the back by the window on the right side. There were about 4 other passengers on the bus. The bus arrived at Gallery Place Chinatown two stops ahead. Few more passengers got on it. One of them was a young man who walked all the way to the back and sat by the window on the left side. He looked like he was probably in his late teens or early twenties. Another young man screaming from outside of the bus jumped inside, run to the back, held the other young man by the neck and threatened to harm him. Other passengers sitting around moved to the front of the bus, probably out of fear. I stood there but refrained from intervening although I was ready to, in case the aggressive young man stroked his victim. He just had his hands tight around the other young man's neck and was uttering threats like " I will kill you if you do this again".

The bus driver did not move the bus until the bully walked away out of the bus back to the bus stop. The driver then closed the bus and pulled out of the bus stop. I checked on the young man at the back of the bus, on the left side of me to make sure he was ok, and told the bus driver that, he should call for help and report the incident. A lady in a wheelchair who was sitting in the front of the bus yelled back at me, "mind your business, he did not hurt him, so there is no need for the bus driver to do anything". I responded that I disagreed with her. She opened the window and shouted something at the young man. He was still at the bus stop, while the bus was halfway to the next stop on 8th Street. He raced from 7th street to the stop on 8th street. The bus was moving slowly, until it reached the stop, and the driver opened the door for folks waiting to get on. The young man got in, stood in the doorway by the driver and threatened to kill me. I hurried from the back of the bus, jumped, and pushed him on the bus driver's wheel, and held on his hand. He had a pouch in his hand, and I assumed he had a gun in there because he was so confident about killing people. I did not want to give him any chance to pull anything out of that bag, whether a gun or a knife. I pushed his head against the bus driver's wheel and pressed all my body weight on him. He was a shorter dude, and I was physically stronger than him. While I had him pinned down on the bus driver's wheel, I insisted that the bus driver call the police. He kept screaming " Get off me, get off me". I told him that I was not going to do that until the police show up. He screamed out for help from his friends

THE YOUNG MAN WHO ATTACKED ME ON THE BUS:

who were at the other station. Three of them raced to the bus, got behind me, and started pulling me off him. One held my neck in a chokehold. I had to free my hand to try to remove my head from the chokehold, but I managed to snatch the pouch from the young man, while he escaped from my grip and made it outside of the bus. The other two of his friends got the pouch off my hand, while I struggled to free myself from the man holding my neck. All of them made it out off the bus and run towards 7th street. I started chastising the bus driver and blaming him for the entire incident. The police showed up about a minute later. They took a statement from me, the driver, and the young victim who I stood for, in the back of the bus. Two officers went to the other station and tried to find the other young man. About five minutes later, they came back and threatened to arrest me if I wanted the other young man arrested. I did not understand their reasoning. They explained to me that when they went to arrest the other man, three of his friends claimed that they witnessed the whole incident, and it was me who assaulted their friend and they came to rescue him from me. The police, therefore, asked both me and the young man to forget the whole incident and move on or both of us were going to get arrested. I told the officers to review the recording of the cameras on the bus and see who was telling the truth. But, there did not want to hear me out. So, I had to do what they asked me to, and they left. The bus driver waited for his supervisors to show up and write an incident report, before the bus continued and dropped me at my destination.

I could have kept arguing with the officers and end up getting unjustly arrested, although all I did was preempt a self-defense move on someone threatening to kill me. But I thought the wise thing to do was to let the officers have their way so I could go to sleep in my bed in my tent instead of in a holding jail cell for the night.

Incidents like these are common occurrences when you live on the street and are around folks who live a life without purpose.

CHAPTER 8:

AN EVICTION NOTICE TO A HOMELESS MAN LIVING OUTSIDE

We were in Fall 2015. I noticed a metal sign post about 20 feet from my tent. It was dark. I had just got to my tent in the bushes from downtown. I approached it and read what it said:

"NOTICE

The district of Columbia will conduct a general clean-up of this area

ON AND AFTER

After the date above this area will be designated as clean and may be cleaned again without additional notice. All personal belongings visible from this location, not removed from this public space by the date, and time listed above, shall be cleaned, and disposed of at any time after the above stated cleanup time. Personal belongings, in plain sight, considered to be of obvious value (i.e., significant personal documents such as ID's. driver's licenses, passports, photographs, financial records, and other similar documents) will be temporarily placed in storage and can be claimed in person within 30 days, by contacting The Department of Human Services at 202 698 4170.

FURTHER INFORMATION AND ASSISTANCE CAN BE OBTAINED FROM:

The department of Human Services 202 698 4170

The Community Partnership at 202 543 5298 ext.101

The Washington Legal Clinic for the Homeless at 202 328 5000

What was I going to do? I did not want to go to a shelter. I thought maybe I should move to a more secluded spot. The only possible location I thought about was too deep in the woods and could be too dangerous. I had seen a herd of deers going in and coming out of there. I had no idea what other wild animals did roam in there.

I decided not to go anywhere but take my tent down every morning, stash it and my belongings in the surrounding woods and raise the tent back up at night when I returned.

I did that for a couple of weeks. I discarded my trash in oversize black plastic trash bags and piled them on the side of the top part of the little bridge eighty feet away. They were never moved. That is how I knew that no cleaning crew ever came there.

EVICTION NOTICE TO A HOMELESS MAN LIVING OUTSIDE

I got comfortable one Tuesday and did not go anywhere. I was up all night the night before and slept in the tent all day that day. I heard a car horn blow at around 4:00 pm. The lady working with the mayor's office in charge of homeless outreach called my name. She had come over to my spot before. She was parked by the bridge. I walked to her car. She told me that a cleaning crew with a truck will come to clean the area and remove everything on the premise, and in sight, including my tent. I felt depressed when I heard that. I told her that I would remove all my belongings and my tent from there before Thursday morning.

Before she drove away, she let me know that technically, the city will not remove my tent and throw my stuff from there after November 1, the start of the winter season. I guess, they do not evict people in the winter. I did not know that it also applied to evicting the homeless living outside.

I was glad that she tipped me off. I just made sure I faithfully took my tent down and stashed all my belongings in the thick woods across the street, no later than 7 am every morning and set it back up, no sooner than 7 pm until a couple of days after November 1st. I never moved the tent after that. I kept it up throughout the winter.

It was a very harsh winter. We had few snow storms. The ground remained covered with snow quite often. I loved it because I was no longer worried about anybody coming to

CHAPTER 9

THE POLICE OFFICER FALSELY ACCUSING HOMELESS MAN OF BREAKING INTO A CAR

On April 20, 2021, Officer Derrick Chauvin was found guilty of second-degree unintentional murder, third-degree murder, and second-degree manslaughter for killing a black man, George Floyd in Minneapolis. The Killing of George Floyd created a greater rage and exasperation that made protests bigger and more widespread. Roads, malls, and other public areas were occupied by thousands of protesters who demanded justice for George Floyd and police reform. The conviction and guilty verdict of Derrick Chauvin shows that, when human beings put their racial identity on the side and see others as humans like them and stand together against injustice, justice is more likely to happen.

What happened to George Floyd, and the rest of the black victims of white police officers almost happened to me. I was fortunate that I did not end up getting killed for no reason by a police officer who seemed to be looking for someone to be his victim.

I had just left the Safeway on New York and 5th street

Northwest. It was open until midnight. It normally stays open 24 hours, until the coronavirus pandemic restrictions were imposed, and people were ordered to stay indoors and come out to shop only for food and other essential needs. I stayed in my tent all day and came out late at night to get what I needed at the Safeway. It was hard to find bread and water, because people used to buy as many of those commodities as they could. I was lucky enough to get about three one-gallon bottles of water. I could not find any bread. But I already had some crackers and tuna cans in my tent. So, water was basically the most important item that I needed.

After I got my stuff, left the store and rode my bike up on New York Avenue until I passed New Jersey Avenue. I got off my bike to take a break from pedaling uphill when I reached 1st Street. I had a long way to go. Most of my trajectory on North Capitol Street was uphill, all the way to my tent. It was probably around midnight. I decided to cross the street and get back on my bike and ride up on New York Avenue and turn left on North Capitol Street till Florida Avenue and get off again and walk up to Rhode Island Avenue, then keep on riding on North Capitol, until I get tired and stop again. The street was dead empty. There was barely any soul out there. Most people were in self-quarantine because of the pandemic. As I was about to cross the street, I saw a car coming on my left side and waited till it passed me. Then I saw another car coming. It was a police car with flashlights on but no siren on.

He was driving fast. He passed me and went to the red light a good block away on North Capitol Street. I started crossing the street when I saw him speeding back in reverse towards me, while I was almost in the middle of the road. He turned his light in my face and said to me, "I've seen you break into a car not long ago", "No, you did not see me break into any car ", I said back. "Yes, I did. I know you. You are always breaking into cars around here. I have family members living on this street block. If one of them ever tells me that their car has been broken into, I will find you." He continued. I started thinking of the black guys that were killed by police in North Carolina and Florida not long before my encounter with that officer. I felt like he was trying to find an excuse to shoot me. I felt so powerless and in great danger. My first reaction was to get to my phone and either call 911 or record him. But he kept looking at me menacingly and kept making threats. Then he held his collar and said, "You know you are being recorded right?" I sincerely doubted that he had his camera turned on. Nonetheless, I said, "good, because your camera will not show me breaking into any car. There are cameras all over this place, so you know that what you are saying ain't true". I felt like he was trying to provoke me and have me say or do something that will be his excuse to shoot me. I asked him to call another officer because I was not feeling safe. He refused. " I am calling 911," I told him, while pulling my phone out of my pocket. He then turned around and sped away. I was trying to turn my camera on and take a videotape of his vehicle, but he was already far away. I dialed 911 and called for help. I explained to the lady who answered the call that I was very scared that this officer threatened me and falsely accused me of breaking into a car. I told her that because of the recent police shooting of innocent black people, I was afraid for my life. I still had to ride my bike up on a dark and empty street to my tent in the woods. I don't know if that officer was going to follow me and hurt me. I was seriously afraid. The 911 lady told me that she understood my fear and that she wanted me to stay on the line until an officer showed up. A white lady officer showed up in no time. I dialed the phone of one of the guys that I met on the street and had been checking on me and helping me at times. I apologized to him for waking him up. But he was glad that I called him. I wanted a witness while I was talking to the second officer. She asked me to describe the officer's car. I did. She told me that it is probably an officer who traveled through the area, and it was not an officer working the area with her. There was nothing else she could do. My friend stayed on the line to make sure that I was safe, while riding my bike to my tent. I told him that I was all right and he could go back to sleep. I rode my bike slowly and kept watching my back, to make sure that the first officer didn't follow me. I turn into and out of alleys to avoid riding straight up to my tent. I got to my tent safely and went to sleep.

Despite that incident, I still believe that there are good police officers out there, and that all of them are not out there trying to kill a black person.

But I believe that there should be police reform and that, the rallies and marches against police brutality were necessary to end police brutality, and specially the killing of black men and women by white police officers.

You should be proud of yourself, If you was one of the young men and women who marched or protested against police brutality and the killing of innocent black men and women all over America. Let's stand for the respect of human life and human dignity and let's end racism. Let's be reminded these words of wisdom spoken at the United Nations General Assembly on October 4, 1963, by the then Emperor of Ethiopia, His Majesty Haile Selassie I, and made famous by Jamaican Reggae Singer, Bob Marley in his song titled war:

That until the philosophy which holds one race superior and another inferior

is finally and permanently discredited and abandoned;

that until there are no longer first-class and second-class citizens of any nation;

that until the color of a man's skin is of no more significance than the color of his eyes;

that until the basic human rights are equally guaranteed to all without regard to race;

that until that day, the dream of lasting peace and world citizenship and the rule of international morality will remain but a fleeting illusion, to be pursued but never attained.

CHAPTER 10:

KICKING THE HOMELESS OUTSIDE IN THE COLD

It was winter of the year 2015. I went to Union Station to fully charge my laptop, so that I could play some chess and listen to videos, when I get back to my tent and stayed sheltered from the extreme cold. It was one of the coldest winter in Washington DC in recent years. It was past midnight when I got inside the station. I thought they would allow the homeless to stay inside during the hypothermia weather. It was a health hazard for homeless people to stay and sleep outside in below freezing temperature. Many of the homeless who had sheltered inside the station to avoid the brutal cold outside were middle-aged and older individuals.

To my surprise, a young security guard and his colleague who was as young as he, walked up to an elderly homeless woman who looked old enough to be their grandmother and ordered her to get out of the station, or he would bar her permanently from the station. He then walked towards other homeless men and women in the main lobby and asked them to leave the station. I took offense when he said to them, "this is not your house here". He told them that there was an emergency shelter van waiting outside, a block away from the station.

He did not bother other people in the station who did not fit the homeless profile. I doubted that an emergency shelter van was waiting at the location he indicated. I had just walked by there on my way to the station.

"They know this is not their house" I yelled at the security guard. "They don't act like they do", he fired back. Obviously, he did not realize that I was homeless. He never asked me to leave. He was only singling out those who looked homeless.

"Come on man, you know that they don't have a home to go to. They are inside here because it is freezing outside. You don't have to be mean to them by the way. They are human beings like you. You never know what can happen to you. You can lose your job one day and find yourself in a situation as bad as theirs. So, stop being so arrogant", I hollered back angrily.

He was visibly annoyed by my reaction. He walked away with the other security guard following behind him.

I got up and headed outside. But there was no van on the corner of Massachusetts and North Capitol Street and anywhere around. The homeless who got put out of the station were standing out there in the frigid cold. I walked across the street to the bus stop to wait for the 80-bus going towards K and 16 Street, North West. One the homeless guy who got put out of the station run across the street and asked me if I had seen the emergency shelter van. I told him that I did not. He was shivering and decided to walk to the closest hypothermia emergency center which was no less than ten blocks away. At least, he could walk such a distance without problem. I was worried about the elderly woman. I doubted she would try to walk in the freezing cold to the next emergency hypothermia shelter 10 blocks away.

I waited in vain for my bus for a good hour. But it was obvious that the buses were not running on their regular schedule because of the winter storm. The emergency shelter van did not show up either. I walked all the way to the 24 hours FedEx store to work on my laptop and keep warm inside.

I was so devastated by the fact that these young security guards did not show any compassion for a homeless woman, old enough to be their grandmother, but would throw her outside in a subzero temperature weather. She could have frozen to death out there. No emergency shelter showed up for the hour that I stood out there.

CHAPTER 11

THE HOMELESS WOMAN WHO WAITED IN VAIN FOR THE SHELTER VAN

She was waiting under the rain for an emergency shelter van. I was riding my bicycle and saw her by the post office, on the corner of North Capitol Street and Massachusetts Avenue. It was late in the evening of March 2024. I doubted that a van would show up that late.

I stopped and asked her if she knew for sure that a van was coming. She answered that she was waiting for the van to go to Harbor Light Shelter, on New York Avenue. "Let me call the emergency shelter hotline to make sure" I told her. I called and told the operator that a homeless lady was waiting under the rain for the shelter van. She told me that she was about to dispatch a van right away. But the homeless lady asked me to hand her the phone. She told the operator that she wanted to go to the Harbor Light Shelter. The operator told her that the shelter she wanted to go to was closed, and that the van will take her to another shelter. But the homeless lady refused to go to any shelter, besides the one she liked but was no longer in operation.

I tried to persuade her to go to whatever shelter the van would take her. But she had her mind made up. I felt sad and hung up the phone. "So, what are you gonna do now? You just gonna stay out here under the rain all night"? I said to her. "I know what I will do. I will go to the hospital. Can you call 911?" She said. "What is wrong with you?" I asked her. "Nothing, I just want to go to stay at the emergency room, so I can be inside for the night" she answered. I told her that she did not need me to call emergency for an ambulance to go to the hospital emergency room to sleep in one of the chairs in there. All she had to do was catch the number 80 bus at the stop right few feet away. The 80 bus would take her close enough to the Washington Hospital Center, although she had to walk a couple of blocks when she gets off the bus.

I felt like calling 911 emergency ambulance for a non-emergency situation was not the right thing to do. She said, she would get on the bus. As soon as she said that an 80-bus showed up at the corner in the opposite direction. "Here goes the bus, right on time", I said to her and started riding my bike down the street. But to my surprise, she did not get on the bus. She stayed under the rain at the same spot. My guess was that she was still under the impression that a shelter van will come to take her to Harbor Light Shelter, although she was told by the emergency shelter van operator, that that shelter had shut down and was no longer in service.

HOMELESS WOMAN WHO WAITED IN VAIN

I felt sad that I could not convince her to get out of the rain and go to a shelter, other than the one she wanted to go to but was shut down. It is very hard to help the homeless suffering from mental illnesses. It was obvious to me that she was one of them.

CHAPTER 12:

HOMELESS MAN WHO HAD A PLACE BUT WAS SLEEPING OUTSIDE

My, friend who was homeless for over 10 years told me that he had finally got his place and was excited to move in the next day. I was so happy for him. He used to sleep in back alleys on the ground for years and now had a fully furnished apartment ready for him.

Two weeks later, I saw him walking to me, when I was sitting in the park across the Washington Convention Center at night. I saw him again walking through the same park at night, about a week after he got his place. He stopped to talk to me and told me that he had just got off the Gallery Place Metro Station and was on his way to panhandle by the clubs on K Street. It was a Friday night. I noticed that he was carrying several bags. "Why are you carrying all these bags" I asked him. "Oh, I brought some stuff to change clothes because I am staying out for the week end, so I can panhandle." I did not understand why he wanted to sleep outside the entire week end. "But you can panhandle and enjoy yourself all night and still go back to your apartment in the morning and come back outside to panhandle tomorrow night. You don't have to sleep outside anymore", I told him. But he told me that he would go back home on Sunday.

A week later, I found out that he had been sleeping outside of the Mc Pherson Metro Station, on the 14th Street side, every night, from the last time I saw him, and he never went back home. I waited another week and walked up to the station at night. He was shivering under a blanket on the floor outside the station entrance. It was freezing cold outside.

I got troubled to see him freezing under a blanket outside in the cold night, while he had a fully furnished one bedroom apartment with a flat TV and the rent and utilities all paid for him.

"Leo, you don't understand. I get bored staying in the apartment by myself. I have been sleeping on the street for too long. I feel more comfortable out here than staying inside an apartment by myself all day. I get depressed staying in there by myself. I feel like the walls are screaming at me," He said. "But you don't have to stay in there all day. You can go in to sleep and come back out in the morning", I responded to him. But my plea to him to give himself a chance by going to his apartment at nights until he gets acclimated to staying indoors fell on death ears.

HOMELESS MAN WHO HAD A PLACE BUT SLEPT OUTSIDE

A month or so later, two other homeless friends of his, started going to his apartment with him. That is how he got used to going home every night.

CHAPTER 13:

RESTAURANT SECURITY NOT LETTING ME USE RESTROOMS BECAUSE I LOOK HOMELESS

I had to use the restroom urgently. I left my books unattended outside and run inside the restaurant right in front of me, as I have been doing over the years, since I have been selling my books out there, long before the 2020 Corona Virus pandemic. Although few homeless, mostly women told me that, they would not let them use the restroom inside, I never had that issue until few weeks ago. A security detail guy of the restaurant, who sees me out here every day and seems cool, shocked me. I am type two diabetic and have not been taking my medication faithfully recently. I have been urinating a lot lately which is a symptom of high blood sugar level. I got up and went inside to use the restroom as usual. As soon as I was about to walk downstairs to the restroom, that security guy singled me out and told me that I could not use the restroom. I asked him why. He said that there were only few urinals working and that since there were a lot of customers in the restaurant, only they, could use them. He did not make any sense to me. It was obvious to me that he made up such a poor excuse to prevent me from using the restroom. I told him that it was an emergency, and that I had a medical condition and could not hold my urine any longer. He told me to go to Cheesecake Factory which was about two blocks away. I told him that I could not leave my stuff outside and could not hold my pee any longer. He then told me to go use the restroom upstairs. I never knew that they had more restrooms upstairs anyway. I just could not believe that he acted like that, although he was always cool with me outside where I sell my books. I just told him not to worry about it. "I'm just gonna pee outside", I said. I came out, grabbed a cup from the trash can and went in the cut and relieved myself, so that I wouldn't urinate on myself. I could not believe it. I always thought he was a nice guy. He always came out and sometimes ask me how business was. I thought he had respect for me. But I see now that he only looked at me as a homeless, because my books are about homelessness. He did not think I deserved to use the restrooms, like the rich customers who go in there. That is not right.

I saw the gentleman the next day when he came in to work, when I was outside selling my books. I told him that what he did the day before was wrong. He was in the rush to go in. It looks like he was late to work. But he said "I'm sorry" as he rushed to get in. I never had any problem with Old Ebbitt's Grill staff and security personnel, past and present, since I have been selling my books outside there for years long before the pandemic. Actually, most of them have been very nice to me. I have been charging my phone inside all the time without any problem. The incident was isolated and only with a particular individual, who have been exchanging nice words with me in the past and have seen me going in to charge my phone and use the restroom multiple times. I don't know why he felt the need to single me out the previous day, while I was heading downstairs like everybody else to use the restrooms. That made me not want to go back to use the restroom in there anymore. I just grabbed a cup from the trash, relieve myself and discard the urine on the grass.

I want you to understand what the homeless go through downtown, although I am no longer homeless. But you can understand how it may be hard for those homeless to find a public place to urinate or even defecate. A day after the incident, I had to catch the bus and go home to defecate. But imagine the men and women who are homeless out there and are given a hard time, when they feel under pressure to go the restroom and are turned away, when they enter the closest establishment with restrooms inside. Don't be shocked when some of them just relieve themselves outside.

CHAPTER 14

I GOT DIAGNOSED WITH TYPE TWO DIABETES

The pandemic had just ended, but people were still socially distancing themselves from others. I could not go and sell my books on the street to pay my rent, while taking my time to write the second book.

I wanted it published the sooner possible. I was on my laptop day and night writing and not getting the proper rest. My vision started getting blurry.

It seems like my vision was deteriorating minute by minute. My mouth was staying dry, and I was thirsty all the time. I was constantly running to the bathroom to urinate.

I realized that something was wrong with me, and that I needed to go the clinic urgently to get checked. But I kept procrastinating because I wanted to finish the book first.

I could no longer see clearly on the screen, what I was typing on the keyboard of my laptop or read anything on a piece of paper.

I panicked and rushed to the clinic the following morning. They drew some blood and tested it. The doctor there told me that my blood sugar level was very high. He decided to give me a shot of insulin immediately and send me to the hospital emergency room right away.

I got worried about that. I did not want to be shot with insulin. I have an aversion for syringe needles being inserted in my skin. I also did not want to become dependent on insulin shots. I was sure there was some pills that he could give me to bring my blood sugar level down, until I get to the emergency room. I was lucky. The nurse could not find the insulin in the clinic.

I don't remember whether he did give me some pills or not. But he did some paper work and asked me if I wanted an ambulance to take me to the emergency room. I told him that I could go on my own to Washington Hospital center on the D8 bus, from the bus stop across the clinic. My tent was located not far from the back of the hospital, although I had a place by then and was no longer living in the tent.

I was so upset and very thirsty. I walked to the CVS store by the Rhode Island Metro station, bought a bottle of water and drank half of it at once. I walked to the station and caught a D8 bus heading to Washington Hospital Center. I got there around 7pm and checked in at the Emergency Room. I waited in a room with other patients for hours. A nurse had me take IV fluids while waiting. She came back and got me around 12 am and sat me in a room by myself. She drew some blood and asked me about the reasons why I came to the Emergency

Room. I looked at her and had no idea what to tell her. I was very confused and disoriented. I could not understand why I could not remember why I came to the hospital. She patted me on my tight and said" I understand". I am glad, I went to the clinic and was sent to the hospital emergency room from there.

My blood sugar level at the clinic was 475. The normal level is between 70 to 100. Anything above 100 is above normal. My blood sugar level was way above normal. I probably could have ended into a diabetic coma, if I had stayed home and did not come to the clinic and hospital on time. The Doctor at the Emergency Room confirmed that I had type 2 Diabetes. He only prescribed me some Metformin 800 pills, plus some other medication, also pills.

He told me that I did not need to be put on insulin. He also made an appointment with the ophthalmologist at the Washington Hospital Center eye clinic. I went there few days later and had my eyes checked. The eye Doctor told me that my vision was blurred because of swelling of my pupils caused by high level of sugar in my blood. He also said that I did not have diabetes in my eyes. I don't know what that meant, but I felt relieved. He told me to get some reading glasses until the swelling comes down, then come back to have some glasses prescribed to me.

I was very sad and disappointed to have become diabetic. The doctor that I saw at the clinic a couple of weeks later told me, that I could reverse the Type 2 Diabetes if I observe a strict low carb diet and lose weight. I was weighing around 270 pounds.

This meant no more ice cream, juices, sodas, pastries and sugary and starchy food. I also was prescribed some blood sugar or glucose monitoring device. It was hard for me to stick myself with anything that looks like a needle. But I had to do it to get some blood off my fingers to check my sugar or glucose level. I was able to do it once I did it the first time.

It seems like more and more men and women of my age are contracting type 2 Diabetes. I am not surprised. Everything we eat has either sugar or salt in it. The Sodas, juices, cookies, cakes, and ice cream that we consume daily are poisoning us. I used to drink a lot of juices and sodas. Now I am paying a higher cost for pouring all that sugar in me.

evict me and throw my tent and possessions away. I was already homeless. I did not have much, but I valued the little bit I had. I did not want the few clothes I had to be thrown away. My tent was my house although it was nothing compared to living in a real house. I had a mattress and box spring inside.

The lady from the Mayor's homeless outreach office showed up with a van a few below-freezing nights and yelled my name from the road. "Leo, we came and pick you up to go to the emergency hypothermia shelter. It is freezing cold out here. It is not safe for you to be out here." She implored me. But I never wanted to go anywhere but stay right where I was. I told her the same thing every time. I had two sleeping bags and about ten blankets and comforters inside my tent.

My body heat kept me warm all night no matter how cold it was outside. I got inside both sleeping bags and tossed the blankets and comforters on top of me, while I was lying on the mattress on top of the spring box. I also had the tent covered with tarps and wool blankets to keep it insulated.

CHAPTER 15:

THE MC DONALD CASHIER WHO REFUSED TO SELL COFFEE TO A HOMELESS MAN

I went to get some coffee at McDonald's on 13th and New York Avenue in Northwest, Washington DC. It was an afternoon of Spring 2018 at around 7 pm. It was a little cold outside. I lined up behind two white guys and a black homeless man in front of them. He was covered with wool blanket. The line moved up. The homeless guy was about my age, fiftyish. I knew him from the streets. The lady at the counter was taking the order of the guy before him. He walked up to me and said, "Do you have a dollar and ten cents?". He was holding a twenty-dollar bill. I was curious to know why he needed a dollar and 10 cents, when he had a twenty-dollar bill in his hand. "I am trying to get a cup of coffee, but she don't wanna take the twenty-dollar bill. She says she ain't got no change."

"Nonsense", I responded while putting my money back in my pocket. "She has some change. Get back in line, and tell her that, this is all you got. She can't refuse to serve you because you only have a twenty-dollar bill. This doesn't make any sense." I responded while making some space in front of me and the customer at the counter. When he told her that he could not get some change, she asked him to order more food for her to take his order. He told her that he only wanted some coffee. She reluctantly took the twenty-dollar bill and took his order for a $1.10 coffee and opened a drawer and had no problem getting him the right change. I was homeless and looked homeless because of my untidy appearance.

I was carrying my big backpack on my back also. I had a lot of dollar bills and coins in my pocket. I only wanted a coffee also. It cost $1.10. But I decided to try that lady and see if she would treat me the same way as she treated the homeless man in front of me. I am quite convinced that she would have not refused to take the order of a regular non-homeless person who only had a twenty-dollar bill and wanted to order some coffee. "Can I take your order?" She said to me, "Yes, mam, one large cup of coffee". I said back to her. "Anything else?" she asked. "No, that's all," I responded. "One dollar twenty cents," she said. "No, no, no, I don't have any change. You got to order more food" she raged when I handed her a twenty-dollar bill. I told her that, that was all I had. She told me that she had no change, and that I should order more food for her to take my order. I told her that I only wanted some coffee. She then ignored me and took the order of the customer behind me. I insisted that she takes my order. She paid me no mind. I asked for her manager. At that point, the security officer, walked up to me and asked me what the problem was. I explained to her. After I did, she pointed to a sign on the entrance wall to indicate to me that the store has the right to refuse to serve anyone. I told her that, in that case, I would complain to whoever was the boss above the manager running that store, because I consider such a denial of service, a discrimination, and I would put it on social media to tell the whole world about it. The security guard then told me that I couldn't film inside the store. She claimed the employee refused to serve me probably because I was filming her. I told her that, that was a bogus claim and explained that the cash register employee refused to serve me because I only ordered a $1 coffee for my twenty-dollar bill. The security guard walked away.

The manager was standing next to the cashier. "What is the problem?" she asked me. I explained that her co-worker refused to take my order. But she paid me no mind and went by her business. I pulled my phone out again and told the manager that I would record the incident and put it on social media, to show the world how McDonald's treats certain customers. At that point, the manager said something to the lady, and the lady went ahead and took my twenty-dollar bill and served me. I put my phone back in my pocket and waited for my coffee.

The cashier lady sat the cup of coffee on the counter, instead of handing it to me as she did with other customers. As soon as I grabbed it, the security guard called me by the soda fountain area. "You can't come here anymore after today", she said to me. I responded: "I will come back here anytime I want to. You don't own this store and you can't prevent me from coming here". She kept following me, while I was exiting the store. As soon as I stepped out of the door, she pulled her phone to take a facial picture of me. I pulled out my phone also and tried to take her picture, but she turned back and went inside the store.

I reported the incident by email to McDonald's customer service office. I went by my business and forgot about the whole situation, until another incident happened at the same McDonald's four months later with another cashier. She also refused to serve me because of an incident that I reported earlier. I sent another email again to McDonald's customer service office to complain about this third incident.

Here is the answer I received.

From: McDonald's Response <donotreply@csmcd.net>

Sent: Tuesday, September 11, 2018, 12:02:38 PM

To: leognawa@hotmail.com

Subject: McDonald's Response

Hello Mr. Gnawa:

Thank you for taking the time to share your recent experience at the McDonald's located at 1235 New York Ave NW. As the Customer Service Representative of this restaurant, I hope you will accept my apology for your unsatisfactory visit. I called your contact number twice to speak with you personally, but I was not successful in reaching you.

Our goal is 100-percent customer satisfaction, and my team works hard to deliver fast, friendly, and accurate service to guarantee that each visit you make is a pleasant one. I'm sorry you feel we have let you down. Please be assured, I am following up at my restaurant to address this issue.

Your e-mail serves as a valuable reminder that our customers are our number one priority. We truly appreciate your feedback and again thank you for taking the time to share your experience with us. We hope to have the opportunity to serve you in the future.

Jessie Morrell

McDonald's Customer Service Representative

New York Ave

(703) XXX.XXXX

I never answered that email although I was satisfied that

someone at McDonald's took the time to respond and offer me an apology. To me, this was a resolved issue. But, I went back there a couple of months later and got denied service by the same Hispanic cashier. On Monday, January 10, 2019, I emailed the customer service representative to complain again.

From: Leo gnawa <leognawa@hotmail.com>

Sent: Thursday, January 10, 2019, 3:33:31 PM

To: ----@fecmanagement.net

Subject: Re: McDonald's Response

To Jessie Morrell,

I am reaching back to you because of a new situation that occurred at the same location, where I was again denied service on Monday, January 7th, 2019 by a manager in the store.

I did record most of the incident on my phone and am willing to show it to you, before posting it on YouTube. But first, let me wish you a happy New Year 2019 and thank you for responding to my last complaint.

Unfortunately, there seems to be a serious systematic problem in that store that needs to be addressed and corrected. I am, therefore, really sending this email so that this type of discrimination and denial of services to some people because of their race and social status, ceases.

As a homeless activist and a self-published author (Homeless Lives Matter, on amazon), I do advocate for the respect of the dignity of people afflicted by homelessness and do write about mistreatments and abuses of homeless people. This explains why I take this complaint to heart because I think this is a case exposing the denial of service and discrimination of people who may look like me.

Here is what happened. On Saturday, January 5th, 2019, my friend Lisa called me and asked me to buy her a salad at McDonald's. I told her to meet me there at about 2 pm. Once there, we locked out bikes outside and went inside to place orders. I was hungry. I decided that we eat inside. But the dining room downstairs was crowded. I thought about eating upstairs, but there was a trash structure blocking the stairs. I assumed the upstairs dining room was not open. But my friend and I were following the manager to the area of the store where iced beverages were made. The manager called an old worker who was mopping the floor in proximity. I heard her speak to him and point at a person holding his tray. The old worker walked up to the man and spoke to him, then walked him to the stairs, moved the trash structure, and led him upstairs.

At that point, I understood that they were selectively choosing who they wanted to use in the upstairs room. I whispered to my friend what I had just witnessed and told her that, we should go sit upstairs as well. Though we were still waiting for our order, I decided to go reserve us a table upstairs by the window and come back to help her carry the food upstairs. But as I got to the trash structure that was blocking the stairs in order to make a way, the old worker who was standing nearby, rushed to me and told me that the upstairs was closed. I told him that I had just seen him taking a customer up there. Then he responded that, it was because that customer had purchased some food. I told him that I am also a customer, and I purchased some food also. He asked me to show him my food.

At that point I responded that I did not feel that I had to show him anything, unless he was willing to reimburse me the money I spent for my food. At that point he moved the trash structure back to block the path. I move it back out of my way and told him that he was wrong to only allow white folks upstairs. I went upstairs, chose a table and took my jacket off and freed my hands, since I had a backpack. I came back downstairs to help my friend with the food, and we went to eat upstairs where there were about 5 customers, all of them were whites.

Though I was saddened by what happened, I left the store after we finished eating and did not make much of it. On Monday evening, I decided to take a break from my activities and go get a coffee at McDonald's. I noticed a white person upstairs, while I was locking my bike on the side of 13th Street. I got inside the store and ordered a large coffee from a friendly young lady behind the counter. As she took my order, I asked her if the dining room upstairs was open. I noticed that the trash structure was blocking the stairs again and the same lady manager was running the store. The cashier lady hesitated to give me an answer. She turned to the manager and spoke to her. The manager then told me that the dining room upstairs was closed. I asked her what time they closed. She said "6:30 pm." I told her "but it is only 6:09 pm," and that from outside, I have seen a white customer upstairs. She responded that those upstairs were the last customers allowed upstairs.

At that point, it was clear to me that she was not allowing homeless folks up there, even if they were customers and wanted to go eat their meal upstairs. I told the lady that if I could not sit and drink my coffee in the store, it was no point of me spending my money there, and I stepped out. But as soon as I got outside, I decided to come back and document the incident by recording it on my phone as evidence. So, I went back to the counter in front of the manager and ordered a large coffee. Then, I asked her why she told me that the upstairs was closed, while it was not 6:30, and therefore not allowing me to use the dining room up there. When she noticed that I was recording it on my phone, she asked me if I was recording it, I told her yes, because I wanted to make sure I had a record of the incident.

At that point, she changed the whole story and started making fabrications. She said that I go upstairs to sleep all the time. What she said, was so ridiculous, because I do not come to that McDonald often, and when I do, I rarely consume my order in there. And when I do, it is for a very brief moment. I had no need to stay at that McDonald's for no longer than the time I need to buy a meal or consume it, if I decided to do so inside. Then she kept on with the lies, such as, I leave my belongings upstairs. I was shocked that she will just make up anything to justify what she really does in that store, as far as denying equal access services to black and homeless folks, although she happens to be black herself.

Sorry if this complaint was long, but I hope this issue is addressed and that I and other people looking like me can be served and be allowed to consume our purchased items at any dining room inside the store, like anybody else.

My phone number is (202) XXX XXXX

Sincerely,

Leo Gnawa

I received a call the next day from Jessie Morrell, the McDonald's customer service representative. She asked me if I was willing to meet the McDonald District Manager for the area and the Store Manager together? I agreed and met both at the date that the customer service representative set.

A couple of days later, I went to the meeting a little before noon at the same McDonald's to meet with both the district manager and the Store Manager. They invited me upstairs. As we got up the stairs together and sat at the table set in the corner, the manager spotted a homeless man sleeping in a chair and leaning on a table not far from us. There were customers up there. She woke up the homeless man and told him to leave. He grabbed his stuff and left right away. Both managers went ahead and explained to me that they had problems with homeless people using the upstairs to sleep, as we had just witnessed. I explained to her that it was fair for the store employees to not allow anybody including the homeless to sleep upstairs. But it was unfair for them to assume that anyone who looks homeless or who is homeless, would go upstairs to sleep. But they kept insisting that the homeless were a problem for their customers.

To argue her case, the manager said that the store had a lot of tourists as customers, because it was located a few blocks from the White House, and that their concern for the tourists' safety was the reason why they had to keep the homeless away. I was very shocked to hear that these managers viewed the homeless as a problem instead of an asset.

Obviously, these managers of McDonald's lack awareness of the value of the homeless for their business. They looked down on their most valuable customers, because they are poor homeless people, and cater to folks who look normal, regular, and have more money.

I told her that the dollar bill of a homeless man and homeless woman holds the same value as the dollar of a tourist from out of town. I went further to make my point. I told them that the homeless men and women who were hanging around the area and who, to them were a problem were more reliable, consistent, and regular customers than the tourists visiting the White House. These tourists stopped and consumed there once in their life, before returning to California, New York, Florida, Canada, Japan, Germany, England, Sweden, France, Australia or wherever. The homeless man and woman does come back and forth inside the store to spend all day on coffee or sandwiches, the money they make all day by begging outside.

"Do you know how much money you guys make from the homeless who spend their money here all day long while the tourists are gone?" I told them. The store was staying open 24 hours. So, they had homeless customers 24 hours, including hours when no tourists were around, and when they had low traffic. At the end of the conversation, they agreed with me that their employees should treat the homeless better and not refuse

THE MC DONALD CASHIER WHO REFUSED

to serve them. They agree to take my suggestions into account and treat the homeless as regular customers and not as undesirable customers. I left around 2:00 pm after our two-hour meeting and went back to 15th Street to sell my book on the street.

CHAPTER 16:

THEY SET THE FOOD ON THE FLOOR, I REFUSED IT.

I was selling my books in front of Old Ebbitt's Grill. It was evening. A couple exited the restaurant, walked by me, and dropped the box of their left-over food on the ground in front of me, without saying a word. I am sure in their heart, they meant well. They would rather give their left over to a homeless man, instead of throwing it away.

"I don't want it, take it back please," I told them. I felt disrespected. I feed birds and squirrels sometimes by throwing food at them. Those are animals. Homeless people are not animals. Even if you want to feed them, do so by respecting their human dignity.

They were surprised that I reacted like that. They just picked it back up and walked off. As they walked away, I said to them, "I am not an animal. I am a human being like you. You could have handed me the food, instead of just sitting it on the ground like you were feeding an animal. I am a human being like you." Whether they heard everything I said or not, I am not sure. But I hope they were able to understand that I was offended by the way they gave the food. They did that because this was how they felt about the homeless. In their mind, it was ok to just drop food in front of a homeless person. Some homeless are indeed mentally ill and they can react violently to folks handing them some food. I get that. But I was out, there, selling my books as a homeless self-published author with my books in front of me and two signs by me advertising what I was doing. I did not exhibit any behavior that will make anyone feel afraid to hand me some left-over.

If you want to give your left-over to a poor person, be kind enough to ask them if they want it and, hand it to them instead of dropping it on the ground. I have seen folks sitting down food by homeless people sleeping outside in doorways. And I saw rats coming to try to get the food. Make sure that you let a homeless person know what you giving them, and let them accept or refuse it.

 Some people think it is better to give food to a beggar than giving them money. It is true that some beggars pretend to be begging money to buy food. What happen is that folks who think it is better to give food instead of money to homeless beggars, go inside the restaurant and come back with some food and hand it to the homeless beggar. But as soon as they walk away, the homeless beggar throw the food away or just let it sit on the ground when they are done begging and leave. The food in Old Ebbitt's Grill is not cheap. That means that whoever when to spend $20 on the meal that will end up on the sidewalk on in a garbage can could have instead give the homeless man a couple of dollars and not worry about what he or she does with it.

Another evening, I was out there selling my books, as a homeless self-published author at the same location. A group of four or five men and women handed me their left-over food. Sometimes I did take food out of respect for those who handed it to me, although I didn't need it. But truth of the matter is that I was out there selling my books and making enough money to afford whatever food I cared to eat. "What is it, I asked the man in the group who had his hand stretched towards me with the box of food in his hand." "What does it matter what food it is? Be lucky somebody gives you some food," he interjected while retracting his hand and walking away with the food and his friends. He felt that I should be lucky that he gave me the food, and I should be questioning him about what food he gave me.

I think that is insane that people would think that because a person is homeless, he or she should not be picky about the food handed to them. I am a type two diabetic. I cannot it eat any food. I have to be picky about what I eat. I will get very sick if I eat too much sweet and starchy food. It will make my blood sugar rise. I might end up getting my legs amputated or lose my eyesight or have heart attacks and many more problems with my organs. This is why I asked them what food it was that they handed me. But they did not get it.

They walked back towards the restaurant entrance and handed the food to a homeless man who was shining shoes thirty feet away from me. I asked him what food that was, as he was opening the box. " Some steak" he responded." "I just got some teeth pulled and I can't eat that," I said loudly so that the guys who gave the food could understand why I asked them what food they wanted to give me.

When you give to a person in need, something that you have no use for anymore and want to get rid of but don't want to trash away, at least give it with kindness and not with contempt and arrogance. And also, do not feel like a person should take what you offer because he or she is needy and has no choice but should be grateful to you for giving him or her whatever you offer them. If you offer a rare or medium-cooked steak to an old homeless person, ask yourself whether they have enough teeth in their mouth to eat it. Never look down on a person because he is less fortunate than you. His or her humanity is equal to yours.

Do not feed anybody in need, food that you would not eat yourself, unless you know for sure that they have no problem with it. Make sure that whatever you offer as help will be valued and appreciated and not be thrown away.

THEY SAT THE FOOD ON THE GROUND

Here is an example. Many times, I was in McPherson Park between 15th and Vermont Street, both on K Street in Northwest Washington DC, and witnessed homeless folks feeding baloney and peanut butter sandwiches to pigeons.

They got the sandwiches from the food truck coming there to feed the homeless every evening. Many of the Sandwiches were abandoned on the benches or just thrown in the trash bin, by the homeless after the van left. I am very convinced that the folks handing the baloney and peanut butter sandwiches on those vans would not eat them themselves. The sandwiches seem to have been made and kept in fridges for a long time. You could barely tell the peanut butter from the jelly because the sandwiches were stale.

CHAPTER 17

THE KIDS WHO GAVE ME A $1 FOR A COPY OF MY BOOK

One day, a guy stopped by my book and seemed so interested in my entrepreneurial venture as a homeless self-published author selling his own books on the street corner. He told me that he was a successful businessman and an owner of a factory in South East Asia, precisely, Indonesia, if my memory serves me right. I was a little bothered that he did not buy a copy but was spending too much time trying to teach me a whole business course and tell me how to run mine. I felt distracted by him, because I could not focus on trying to attract customers.

One of the things he was telling me was that, when people come to me with less than the ten dollars that I was asking for a copy, I should just give them the copy. In my mind, I was like, "ok, I am here trying to make a profit off selling a copy, so how dumb does that sound? I might as well just give the copies away if I have to take every short money." But actually, I did take a lot of short money and rarely turned anybody down before meeting this guy.

While I was talking to him, someone stopped and told me that they only had four dollars for a copy. "Take it, take it," the man yelled at me. I went ahead and did it.

It was afternoon. I was selling my books outside. A family walked by me, the man was black, the wife was white, and the kids were mixed. There were young. Maybe 10 and 7. They stopped, picked a copy, look at it, and walked away. Both kids run back to me and handed me a dollar bill. I thanked them. Then each of them picked up a copy. Before they run back to their parents waiting for them, a quarter of a block away, I said, "I am selling them". They put the copies back down. But I felt terrible and told them that they could have the copies. I felt bad for refusing the copies to some kids who were kind enough to give me a dollar. Why couldn't I give them two copies or at least one, as a gift even if they had no money? From time to time, some folks would hand me a twenty-dollar bill for a copy and asked me to keep the change. I was selling the book for ten dollars on the street.

The kids walked back to their parents with the free copies and run back towards me and handed me a hundred-dollar bill. They told me that their parents told me to keep it. I thanked the parents who came back and took a picture with me and the kids holding their copies.

I will admit that I always thought of that businessman, when folks come to me and have no money or less than the cost of the book. I hear that man's voice telling me "Never refuse when they have less than ten dollars, always take it". I can tell you for sure that I gave a lot and received a whole lot more. What you give out is never lost. It always comes back some way, somehow.

THE DEPRESSED GUY WHO GAVE ME $50 SO HE WON'T GO BACK TO THE BAR

One night, a guy came out of the bar, back and forth to smoke a cigarette not far from me while looking at my signs and me every time. I was hoping that at some point he would approach me and get a copy, but that was not happening.

He finally stepped towards me, the fourth or fifth time that he came out to smoke a cigarette. "What are you selling?" He asked me. I went ahead and explained to him that I was a homeless guy, who self-published a book to create awareness about homelessness and was selling it to get a place one day. "

He did not say much. He pulled a fifty-dollar bill out of his pocket and handed it to me and said, "you know what? I have been wasting a lot of money drinking all evening. I am having a lot on my mind, and I am not happy. I am just wasting my money on alcohol, but I still have to deal with the issues bothering me. I'd rather give you have this fifty-dollar bill than me going back to waste it in the bar". I was very sad and did not feel right taking that money, while knowing that the man was going through some tough times. I took the money and tried to talk to him, but he did not reveal much of what issue he was dealing with. I nonetheless found words of encouragement for him and wished him well. He appreciated my compassionate words and left by asking me to pray for him.

THE STRANGER WHO GAVE ME $100 BECAUSE I LOOKED HOMELESS

I was on my way to selling my book. I was on foot because I had a flat tire on my bike. While I was heading to the Safeway store door, a man who had just left the store and was walking towards me, turned back around and started following behind me after he had just passed me. I felt his presence behind me and was very annoyed. I turned around and he immediately told me, "Sorry can I ask you a question?" He said. I had my big bag full of books on my back. "Are you homeless?" He added. "Yes sir". I responded. "Are you homeless for real?" he continued. "Yes, I am, I live in a tent, and actually, I am a self-published author and am going to sell my book titled Homeless Lives Matter. "You want a copy?" I said to him while taking the bag off my back. "No, no, I just want to help you." He said while handing me a $100 bill." "Give the book to somebody else," he said while I was trying to pull a copy out and hand it to him. He then turned and walked back in his initial direction.

CHAPTER 18:

WHO AM I? I AM NOT HAPPY

I wrote this article in a Washington DC Homeless Newspaper called Street Sense.

Street Sense July 15, 2005, by Leo Gnawa:

I want to carry on with the theme of happiness. Many readers responded positively to my column in the May 15 issue, dealing with happiness and success. One e-mail message I received was from a 20-year-old Russian tourist, who had just set foot on American soil when I first met her. Her correspondence puzzled me. She wrote, "You're much happier than many people who have everything except themselves. happiness is just a state of mind regardless of your possessions."

State of mind? I think she's right. If someone has more than enough for their daily sustenance, to maintain a stable life and to meet all their material needs, and he or she still cannot find happiness, something's wrong. I will be honest: If I had the wealth, the talent, and the fame of Michael Jackson, I would be happy, and I don't care what anyone says. I am just being real.

Someone said that money is the root of all evil, but I beg to differ. I think money is all right, there is nothing wrong with money. The roots of all evil are in man's motives based on greed, selfishness and insensitivity towards others. Money is a tool just like a knife but in the mind of whoever uses the knife – same as money.

As I have stated in my previous column, my present condition is that of unhappiness because of my failure to achieve my ideals. Consequently, it is my belief that my quest for happiness can become fruitful only when I achieve success in turning dreams into reality. And all I can dream of now is material and financial stability. So, I wonder how folks like Michael Jackson do, with all their wealth and success, end up unhappy that they're engaging in weird behavior.

I have no clue what the answer is. But, when I read my young Russian friend's e-mail again, I can see an answer. She said, "You are happier than most people who have everything except themselves."

She's got a point. The truth of the matter is that I am much happier than Michael Jackson because now I would not want to be in his current predicament – despite his recent "not guilty ruling." But being accused of child molestation and having the reputation of a pedophile wouldn't make anyone happy except a psychopath. No wonder Michael flew to Bahrain, in the Arabian Peninsula with his three children right after the verdict of the child molestation trial, in what appears to be a self-imposed exile out of the United States.

What transpires from the Michael Jackson situation is that the identity crisis, which he obviously suffers from as his metamorphosis from one race stigmatized as inferior to another held as superior shows, has not allowed him to fully enjoy his good luck. By good luck, I mean talent, fame and wealth.

I am not a psychiatrist, and I will not attempt to explain Michael Jackson's mind. I understand that he has allegedly been subjected to some abuse as a child. So, this may be the reason of his problem with identity. Some say he is still a child trapped in the body of an adult, he believes he is Peter Pan (a fictional little boy character who refuses to grow up and enjoys performing magic).

However, it is obvious that Michael Jackson's identity crisis has impeded the happiness that should have been naturally resulted from his success in the universal world of music, entertainment, and business. The lesson I see in this situation is that at some point we have to accept who we are and the way we are. It is better to be happy with what we have than to pursue an unattainable dream and, in the process, cause greater damage to our mental stability and our self-esteem. We can cause ourselves a lot of misery by just trying to be what we are not.

There is a lot of wisdom in what my Russian friend wrote me. I may not have anything as far as material things. But, I have me, myself, and I. As long as I keep consciousness of my integrity, then I can improve my condition sometimes in the future. Sometimes we are so focused on what we perceive as the negative part of us that we fail to appreciate the good side of us. Until we learn how to love ourselves sand accept ourselves, we cannot be happy – even if we have everything. The dissatisfaction with self will always prevail over the gratification with wealth, as is the case with Michael Jackson. When we know ourselves, we know that no matter how bad we see things within or around us, there is also something good within and around us, too.

I am not happy to be poor and homeless, and as long as that is what I identify with, I will not be happy. But despite homelessness, I still have my personality and I am quite sure there is something good in it. I should be happy I have me because there is something good in me and in all of us.

Leo has been a Street Sense vendor for four months. If you would like to send him any comments, please e-mail him at leognawa@hotmail.com.

CHAPTER 19

A HOMELESS MAN SURVIVAL IN THE WOODS THROUGH THE CORONA VIRUS PANDEMIC

You must learn how to survive and make the best out of the worse of situations. That is what I used to tell myself when things got rough.

In 2020, Washington DC like the rest of America was shut down because of a pandemic caused by the Corona Virus. Thousands of people were dying after being sickened by the highly infectious illness.

On March 30, of that year, Mayor Bowser declared a state of emergency for the District. I was totally caught off guard. I had no idea how I was going to make any money, since I could no longer sell my books on the street. I was less afraid about catching the virus and more concerned about how I was going to survive. I wondered what I would do, after the stay-at-home order was going to go into effect on April 1.

The order stated that: "Residents may only leave their

residences to engage in essential activities, including obtaining medical care that cannot be provided through telehealth and obtaining food and essential household goods, to perform or access essential governmental functions, to work at essential businesses, to engage in essential travel and to engage in specific recreational activities that the order defined. Anyone found to be violating the order would be charged with a misdemeanor and subject to a $5,000 fine and/or 90 days in prison."

I sincerely doubted that the police would arrest homeless people who had no home to stay in and would therefore be in violation of the stay away order. Nonetheless, I was in a total state of confusion. I was not so concerned about catching the virus, but more worried about how I was going to make any money to survive. I could no longer go sell my books on the streets. The Pandemic was a perfect example of how I was able to see a problem as an opportunity to achieve something better than the predicament I was in.

I decided to use the internet and social media to sell my books, since I could no longer make any money on the streets. I got Brad to help me build a website. Brad was a good Samaritan. I met him when he was looking for a homeless man to give him a jacket that he promised him, when he saw him earlier in the day but did not find him, when he came back with it to the place where they were supposed to meet. I named it homelesslivesmatterbook.com. But the website alone was not enough to attract viewers. I started and built an Instagram page and named it homelesslivesmatterbook. I attracted followers and grew my audience fast by posting daily on how I was surviving through the pandemic every day.

Here is what I posted on it daily to document chronologically, how I survived during the covid pandemic shutdown.

May 2020

-Coronavirus outbreak is making life harder for the homeless because everything is shut down. But in my tent, I use my imagination to create a meal that is healthy but cheap and easy to make.

-My meal of the day. Avocado mixed with Tuna in oil, mayo, ketchup, hot sauce. And organic fruit spread mixed with peanut butter. And Ritz crackers ha ha. I am surviving the best I can in isolation.

-The Laundromat where I normally wash my clothes, has been shut down since the Coronavirus outbreak.

- I figured out that I could spread my larger tarp on the grass and capture some rainwater last week when it rained for a couple of days. Then use the rainwater to wash my clothes and dry them the next day when it was sunny.

-The other day, two security officers came and told me that I could not be here. But hey, I am back again. I got to write. Public libraries are closed, because of covid 19. But I still got to write my next book. The hell with covid 19. It ain't gonna stop me from writing wherever I can find a place to keep my laptop charged.

-I am feeling a little stressed. It is 7:24 pm. This is my meal for the entire day. Just two cans of tuna with mayo and some herbs and spices seasonings and some strawberry fruit spread on the side. And some mountain dew. I normally don't consume that much soda drink, but once in the blue moon. I am here in the woods, trying to survive the best I can until this Coronavirus nonsense go away and everything gets back to normal.

-My meal of the day. Tuna and mayo with some spices and crackers again. Yes, it is depressing to eat the same thing over and over and over again every day. But hey, it is healthy, and I will not starve during this pandemic shut down. I can survive on the tuna and crackers u till things get back to normal. I stay right here away from everybody, so I won't worry about catching Coronavirus. I can't afford to get sick. So, I am here in the woods (not totally) and surviving on the little food I got here. I am grateful.

-Just took a hot shower at the Downtown Day Services Center for the homeless, located inside the New York Ave. Presbyterian Church at 1313 New York Ave. NW. I had to make a reservation on Tuesday to be able to take a shower today. I am glad they are still doing showers

A HOMELESS MAN SURVIVAL IN THE WOODS THROUGH PANDEMIC

although on appointment even though they are not providing all the services as usual and only allowing inside the building, whoever has an appointment for shower or laundry.

-The days I got to wait till I can make it to a hot shower, I just go get a gallon or two of water at a corner store about 7 blocks down the street and shower right outside my tent. I don't care how cold the weather and the water are, I got to shower every day. Being homeless doesn't mean that you got to forget about your hygiene. No excuse not to clean your body every day. Sorry. I got to.

-Hey, I also had to wash my clothes. The Laundromat where I normally do my laundry is not open back yet cause of Coronavirus restrictions. Cause I am homeless doesn't mean I got to feel comfortable wearing dirty clothes. It is always a way, no matter what. We always got to try to find a solution to any issue we face. If I am not giving up. You shouldn't. Stay blessed, whoever you are.

-I stashed my little bucket, body wash, and lotion in these bushes. Wow, they are still there. About to take a quick shower outside here while the streets are still deserted. I had to ride 20 minutes down here to be able to shower outside here before I start my day. Need to be fresh to start a new day with a clear mind. No matter what you go through, stop complaining. No need to depress yourself. Just do what you got to do to feel better.

-Blake and Sarah, two strangers I met on Instagram, cared enough to bring me 17 gallons of water and some packs of Tuna and crackers. I don't know how to thank them enough for taking their precious time and drive all the way up here to give water to a 55-year-old homeless man living in the bushes. I am so touched; I don't know what to say.

JUNE 2020

-I got soaked last night on my way back. Once here, I spread a tarp and captured rainwater. I am filtering it in a 3-gallon bottle and will add a bit of alcohol to disinfect and use it to clean up. I saved the rest for the future, so I won't use my drinking water for hygienic purposes. Always try to make the best of the situation even on a rainy day. Rainwater, free water. Use it.

-I am watering my tomato plants with rainwater I captured and saved a couple of days ago. Even a homeless person can grow food. All you need is a slice of tomato with grains in it and some soil. Water is free from the rain. Just figure a way to capture when it rains and save it in empty water bottles. Where there is a will there away.

-We are still in phase 1 opening here in DC (Coronavirus pandemic restrictions). If you have washing and drying machines in your house or your building, consider yourself blessed. It is people outside here who have to go through headaches to get their clothes washed. Enjoy your blessings and don't complain about insignificant things. Somebody out here is doing worse than you. Don't worry. Be happy.

-I Spread a tarp on the ground to collect rainwater to use to shower. Homeless or not, no excuse, I still got to wash my behind. Free water from the sky. For every situation, there is a solution. Just take your time and figure it out. Survival is a must. Don't stress.

-I am riding my bike by this woman sleeping under scaffolds by an apartment housing construction site at 3:00 pm under 83-degree temperature.

-Laundromat closed earlier. Couldn't make it. Had to hand wash few clothes items to have some clean to wear till I get to laundry tomorrow. As I always remind all of you, there is always some kind of solution to a difficult situation. So don't let any problem stress you. Yes, I am in downtown Washington dc handwashing my clothes. So, what if somebody sees me? Can't let pride and shame get in the way.

-I stashed a laundry bag filled with dirty clothes and a bottle of Gain detergent in these bushes here in downtown Washington DC, till tomorrow when I am finally able to get to the laundromat up the street. I am not worried about anybody stealing my dirty clothes. If they do, then they must really need it. I won't be mad.

July 2020

-I Just took a nice shower outside my tent. Feeling fresh. About to go *downtown ship few more books and take care of business. Forget my issues, worries, or problems. I got to stay focused on turning this day into a productive day, by the time I get back here late in the night. If you have not ordered your book yet, what you waiting on? Come on, we all got to eat! Haha. Stay blessed.*

-I came to my friend's apartment for a night. I give him $20 for a night whenever I decide to come here to feel in a cool place and escape the heat in my tent.

-I want to express my gratitude to Laney for dropping a cooler, some ice, and some water by my tent a few minutes ago. Thank you so much to all of you who take some of your time to show compassion for the homeless. Thank you again, Laney (laneybogs08). Stay blessed

-Before I left this morning, I opened the tent wide to let everything dry. I am back before the rain forecast for 7:00 pm starts. I made sure I checked the weather this morning and got back here in time. When I got back here last night after the storm, the floor of my tent was flooded. I emptied the water in a bucket and will use it to water my tomato plants. Surprisingly, my tent-top mattress was not soaked. I had a peaceful sleep.

-When I came back the night before Yesterday, my tent was flooded. I did not look at the water on my tent floor as a problem. I collected it and fill a 7-gallon water jar plus another water gallon bottle and save all that water for my tomato and garlic plants. It had been really hot

lately and the plants were dying until the storm breaks these last two days. But the heat may resume soon and at least I got water saved for the plant. Water may look dirty because dirt may have got in, but the plants will benefit from it. A lesson of the day, turn a problem into a solution, maybe not for you but someone else or an element of nature.

-Came to my buddy's place to take a long cold shower. On my way back to my tent before rain starts. Finding a place to take a shower can be a headache for the homeless, mostly for women out there.

-Got my tent covered this time. Rain started. The lesson of the day. Always be prepared mostly for predictable situations. If you don't then the calamity that comes your way will be self-inflicted. Learn that lesson from the last time when I did not check the weather forecast and left without covering my tent and came back to find the tent flooded.

August 2020

-It is 5:30 am. I feel very hungry. Just got some mocha, a can of tuna salad snack, and two bananas from 7/11. I woke up around 3:30 am to some noise outside my tent. When I peeped through the screen, I saw a pair of eyes shining in the dark outside towards me. I thought of either a cat or a raccoon. Most probably a raccoon. Anyway, when you sleep outside, you are subjected to be awakened constantly by all *sorts of noises and the abrupt presence of animals or humans in your immediate surrounding.*

-I was blessed by Yoojin and her friends. They just brought me a small table and a chair. Now I can write in my tent. I broke the chair I had and with no table and chairs, it is very hard to write inside a tent. I want to express my gratitude to Yoojin and her friends. Thank you so much

-It rained abundantly the previous couple of days. As some of you already know, I do collect rainwater as I am doing this morning and filter it and use it for personal hygiene or to water the tomatoes and garlic I am growing around here. I am not drinking it though. I could not make it to a shower place, so I have to shower out there. I wear long shorts that reaches my knees, so I won't be accused of indecent exposure, although no pedestrians are walking by and the cars on the road cannot see me because I am behind my tent. There is no human habitat or business around here. It is only nature and peace and quietness. So, I am not bothering anybody.

-I am about to go to sleep on somebody's couch tonight with a fan blowing right above my head in this old building with a ceiling fan barely blowing some air and with no air conditioner. Though I prefer my bed in my tent to a couch, I am still grateful that my friend opens his doors to me to come inside anytime I feel the need to come inside. At least I can sleep tonight without hearing insects and birds making all sorts of noises all night, haha. Anyway. Hopefully, I wake up in

the morning to see another day.

- Just waking up on somebody's couch. Kind of missing my bed in my tent. Sleeping on a couch gives me neck pains that I don't need now. Haha. But I am grateful that somebody opened their door to me for a night and in exchange, I could also help them with $20 that they can use since they are also poor.

-8:00 am. Riding my bike by this homeless man sleeping in the median lane during heavy morning traffic on one of Washington DC's busiest highways. Seems like homelessness is getting worse. Anybody paying attention?

-9:45pm. I had gone to my tent, a couple of hours ago. But because of the rain these couple of days, it seems like the whole area around my tent is infested with mosquitoes. It was a little stressful to have to deal with the humidity and mosquitoes. So, I called my friend and asked if I could come and sleep on his couch for tonight. He said yes. I made a stop at the Giant store and got myself some stuff to cook while I am here for the night. I got dishwashing soap since I know he had a little bottle the last time I was here and most likely he had run out. I gave him $20 as usual for a night.

-4:13 pm. I am walking by a cemetery and feeling like it is the place to rest in peace after suffering so much in this life. But no rush, hahaha. We all gonna end up there. Until then, I can only try to feel ok even when feeling depressed.

-7:00pm. I just woke up in my tent after taking a nap when I came back from returning to my friend's place to pick up my solar charger that I forgot when I had come to my tent the first time this afternoon. When I return here and rest on my bed, I fell into a deeper and restful sleep than sleeping on a couch. Many homeless do not get appropriate sleep because they don't sleep on a comfortable bed. So, one thing I made sure of is to have brought a bed here in my tent. Although it is better to be indoors than outside, at least I got this bed here which makes sleeping out here more restful.

-10:10am. Left my tent at 8:00 am. Got to SOME and took a shower by 8:45 am. Now I am having breakfast (and most likely my only meal of the day) outside on a bench. Having fried croaker fish with fried eggs and home fries and bread a grape jelly and Iced tea lemonade mix. All for $10.20 from carry-out on New York and New Jersey Ave. in North West DC. My book is my source of income. It allows me to eat what I want.

-9:15 am. Another frustrating start today. I left SOME at around 8:50 am. I went there to take a shower. I left my tent at 8:20 am. I got to SOME at 8:32 am. I was the only one standing outside at the door for a shower. On the door, the sign says "Men showers from 6:00 am to 9:30 am and women Showers from 9:45 to 11:30 am.
-I decided to let the gentleman doing the showers know that I was waiting. I opened the door and saw him talking in the dining room with other workers. I waited till he stepped out of the dining room and

told him that I was waiting to take shower. He told me that the two homeless in showers were the last ones for the day. I closed the door and asked a lady outside what time it was. She told me 8:42 am. I opened the door back and asked another worker to call the supervisor for me. The gentleman steps back from the showers area as the lady supervisor walked towards the door. The gentleman stood right behind her. I asked to talk to her alone. He responded, "you gonna talk about me, so I want to hear". I asked to talk to her in private. She asked me to meet her in front of the building. I did but she never came. I returned to the entrance door. The gentleman stood there. I told him, I just want to make suggestions to her for some changes in the way this shower thing is run because it is so frustrating to come there at 8:38 am and be told that the shower is done for the day when the sign says showers end at 9:30 am. Then he changed the story. "you came here at 8:45 am and I told you that you might not be able to make it to the showers", he said. I told him that I talked to him at 8:38 am and he told me showers closed for the day after those in there come out. I got on my bike and left.

The real issue here is that the gentleman is lazy and doesn't care about the homeless waiting to take a shower. He normally sits at his desk and spends the entire time on his cellphone instead of monitoring the time each person spent in the shower so that the next person waiting can get in. Then he rushes to close the shower early. And he never clean showers after last used, for the next person. Things like that frustrate and discourage many homeless people from taking showers at places offering service to the homeless.

-1:30pm. I am back in my tent downtown. About to eat this meal that this lady cooked for me. Every Sunday, she fixes me a meal and I go pick it up by the senior citizen building where she lives. She is one of my angels. At least I know, every Sunday someone cares to make sure I got a home-cooked meal.

September 2020

-6:35 pm. I Just got to my tent. I am being attacked by millions of Mosquitos. It rained for the last couple of days that I was away. And I am being bitten left and right. They just invaded the whole area cause it is still wet. I think I am going back to my friend's place in North East.

-8:15pm. I came by Safeway to meet albaptist08 who brought me some comforter and pillows after I posted earlier about going to Forman Mills to get some blanket. Now, I don't need to worry about purchasing a blanket. It is a bit chilly outside here and I am getting on the bus to head to my tent. Thank you so much to Alex and all the angels out here who care for the homeless.

-10:20pm. I am in some downtown Washington DC back alley loading dock, charging my phone before heading to my tent for the night. Another homeless man sleeping in the doorway.
-11:00am. I am just waking up and about to take a cold shower outside my tent. It was chilly throughout the night. The cover I received from

albaptiste08 kept me warm. Thank you again, Alex. You are an angel.

-4:46 pm. I am checking on some of the tomatoes I planted a few months ago around me as an experiment when the coronavirus epidemic started, and everything got shut down. I had planned to grow food in the woods in case things had got worse and food scarce. When toilet paper, then water, then bread shelves started getting empty as stores, I had to think of plan B in case the shortages had extended to major food items, and everybody started looking for food. Haha. Homelessness has tough me a lot about survival. You got to think ahead instead of panicking when uncertainty shows on the horizon. That is one of the things I am writing about in my next book.

October 2020

-4:30 pm. Another Angel, by the name of Faith, found a bike for me from her circle of bike riders. She asked around if someone had a free bike, and here we. She drove her hour away to bring me this bike. I am so amazed and humbled by the kindness and support I am getting from many of you reading my posts here. Thank you, a lot Faith, for this bike. It will help a great deal during this period of the coronavirus pandemic. At least I don't have to worry about public transportation. A bike will take me anywhere. I am grateful.

HOMELESS PEOPLE ARE HUMAN BEINGS TOO

-12:06 PM. *After sleeping on someone's couch for a week, so that I could be indoors, away from mosquitoes, I am finally back in my bed. But my bed outside, in a tent of course. More comfortable than a couch, though. But sleeping on somebody's couch inside a house is preferable to doing so on a comfortable bed outside. I am not trying to glamorize the homeless by any means. But I can sleep and see something enjoyable in every situation, good or bad. So, I am gonna enjoy this bed and not the fact that it bothers me because it is outside. I am grateful.*

I am Charging my portable power with my solar charger right by the tent in nature. One of the Angels who have supported and helping for a long time, got it for me when the pandemic started so that I could be safe and not worry about coming downtown to charge my phone. I receive so many blessings from total strangers and I am grateful for that. I also feel it as a duty to use the extra I get to also help those around me in dire need, whenever I can.

-*Me fooling around with this praying mantis climbing on my bike. I just love observing these beautiful little creatures in this natural environment, which they don't mind sharing with a homeless man. We need to stop destroying the environment, which is their natural habitat, otherwise, these beautiful creatures will become extinct.*
-*Haha. Sometimes, I feel safer around animals, wildlife, trees, and plants. Human beings are the most dangerous creatures on this planet. This is why we all need to contribute to increasing*

compassion, empathy, and respect for our fellow humans.

NOVEMBER 2020

-12:00am. Stopping by the cemetery on my way back to my friend's place. I believe that I am on this earth for a purpose and that I am not gonna be here forever. So, stopping by a graveyard helps me appreciate life even in the predicament I am and understand that time is pretty short.

-I am here with the crowd at the White House today Saturday, November 7, 2020, witnessing history taking its course. The first woman elected Vice-president of the United States. I also came across this homeless brother. Not a Trump supporter. I don't agree with his choice of some of the words he used to refer to Trump. But those words are street vernacular. But today, after a long depressing wait, a winner was declared by the media. some are happy, others are not. This is Democracy. Somebody wins, somebody loses. But life goes on. We still got to love one another.

-5:50pm. I got the tent set back up. I didn't nail it to the ground very tight the last time I left. I will be back tomorrow morning to take everything out and mostly the mattresses and let them dry all day. I might have to spend tomorrow night on my friend's couch because I *need to let the inside of the tent dry out. Some rain got into it. But that's my fault. I didn't plan to be gone for so long*

-I came to pick my Thanksgiving dinner from Yesterday. This will also be my birthday dinner. This nice lady that I have known from her from Franklin Park in NW Washington DC, where they use to feed and hand out hygiene stuff and clothes the Homeless. Her name is Arlene. When the Coronavirus pandemic shut everything down, I could no longer make money selling copies of my book, Homeless Lives Matter, Homeless My Story, on the street. Though I had lost touch with her, she reached to me to check on me and offered to cook a homemade meal for me every Sunday. The last Sunday, I met her, she told me she was gonna have a Thanksgiving dinner for me. When she called Yesterday, I slept in the day after I spent nearly 24 sleepless hours getting book orders ready. So, I did not have Thanksgiving dinner Yesterday. I am about to enjoy this meal prepared by this angel. I feel so blessed to have all these angels around me. I believe that angels are a real human being that shows up on your path at the right time to bless you unexpectedly. I am so great that despite all the miserable experiences I have been having, there are still great human beings out there who can empathize without casting judgment.

-5:03pm. I am outside on a bench by the bushes where I stash my dirty clothes until I take them to laundry nearby. I decided to spend my birthday outside so that I can remind myself that I am still homeless, although I have been able to go indoors and sleep on my friend's couch or floor for a couple of weeks. I will be heading to my tent to meditate

and reflect on my journey so far. Seems like I am seeing some light at the end of the tunnel, but I am still conscious of my current homeless situation while working hard to end it permanently. I have been homeless off-on for a long time. But now, with my writings, doors are opening. I am grateful. I am not complaining. This meal is delicious, blessed be the sister who prepared it out of compassion and pure kindness. Leo

DECEMBER 2020

-2:00pm. I made my appointment with the dentist at SOME dental clinic for the homeless. Time for dentures. Last year, I had about 10 teeth pulled. I was in the process of getting dentures when the Coronavirus pandemic shut everything down. So, I am getting back with the process and hopefully, I will be able to properly chew again and eat some of the food I like but can't eat now. I am glad I can my book and buy my own food so that I won't rely on food from soup kitchens that may not be able to properly digest. I am grateful. While at the same time, I want to let you know that dental care although available for the homeless in Washington DC, is still a concern. Hopefully more homeless have access to dental care. And I am grateful for places like SOME dental clinic here in Washington DC. They doing a good job.

FEBRUARY 2021

-The air outside is so fresh and pure. I feel like in heaven walking outside in the snow. Tomorrow is another day. Hopefully, tomorrow will give birth to good news. Hopefully, I wake up to see tomorrow. We shouldn't take anything for granted in this life. Every second we are still here on this earth is something we should be grateful for.

-Some angel is willing to rent me an apartment. Thank you to everyone who supported me and my book. I have saved as much as I could so I would no longer have to sleep outside or on somebody's couch or floor. I am grateful to you all. Although it is not finalized yet, I am in the process of renting an apartment from a landlord, who is willing to rent to a homeless man who only relies on selling his book as an income. I call this a miracle.

-Tomorrow I am picking up keys for my apartment. I just signed the lease and will pick the keys tomorrow. There are fixtures to be made on Monday. But I will be working on getting some furniture this weekend. Landlord asked for the first month and security deposit. I went ahead and paid first and last month's rents plus security deposit, therefore 3 months of rent.

-5:00pm. Sleeping in my own bed, in my own place is so therapeutic. I feel like I am in a hospital recuperating. Wow, my whole body and mind are feeling the effect of real rest and relief and healing.

CHAPTER 20

WORDS OF INSPIRATION

I shared the following thoughts daily on my Instagram page to encourage myself and my readers whenever I felt stressed, depressed or anxious about anything as a homeless person. Hopefully, some of those thoughts inspire and motivate you. The whole purpose of this book is to inspire and motivate you:

One day, I left my tent, walked my bicycle on the grass until I got to the sidewalk of the road. I got on my bicycle and starting pedaling until I noticed a plant growing out of the concrete-covered ground of the sidewalk. This is a lesson for all of us getting stressed over the adversities we are facing. Never give up, you can still make a way through, even in the most hostile environment.

-Sometimes, it feels like the more obstacles you remove out of your way, the more pile up and obstruct your path. Don't relent, keep trying even harder until things get better for you.

-Patience can be stressful. But please don't give in to desperation. When you know that you are putting the right efforts into the right actions and that you have realistic expectations, just be patient and keep doing the right thing. Don't give up trying. Leo

-Don't depress yourself over your problems, Focus more on how you can humble yourself and seek help and use the help to create opportunities for yourself to make things better.

-Spending too much of your time worrying about your problems will only cause you stress and depression. Focus instead on how and what to do to solve them and you will be motivated.

-Some of your folks don't want to see you happy. It seems like they love to see you going through hell and whatever they can do to make it worse for you, they will. Don't let it get to you. Be grateful to those who care about you.

-Sometimes strangers will show more compassion to you than your own relatives and close acquaintances, who will for no reason just act wicked towards you.

-I'd rather be a lonely poor homeless bum living in the woods in peace and harmony with nature and getting along with trees, birds, insects, than being around human beings who love drama and love being unhappy and miserable.

-I just believe that we should all be longing for peace and happiness. Otherwise, what is life worth if you have a good job, a roof over your head, a nice car, money in the bank, but want to be unhappy?

-I am not here to judge anybody, but it is obvious to me that some people just like to be miserable and make everybody around them miserable. I don't know what kind of gratification anyone will feel out of creating unhappiness inside their soul and around them.

-I cannot tell you how shameful and sad I have felt about my life as a homeless person. Even talking about it publicly is disgusting, to tell you the truth. I don't feel any pride coming up here and showing you another person's couch or living room where I sleep or kitchen where I cook my meal or a tent in the woods where I sleep. But, I can overcome those bad feelings and look at the greater picture, of how sharing my story can inspire and motivate so many of you and also create awareness about Homelessness and the reality of some of us who suffer from it.

-You will make mistakes and errors or face situations that will mess you up and cost you. Don't panic, don't be discouraged, and don't be angry at the whole world. Just pay the cost, learn from what went wrong and do better next time.

-Every homeless man or woman deserves a roof over their head whether or not they can afford it. No human being should be denied their human rights a house and even if they are poor and don't have enough money. I know the trauma and humanity of dwelling outside. I am still suffering from it.

-If you get stressed out very easily because of every hurdle on your path, you aren't going to get far or anywhere on your journey. Just relax, and figure out a way to go around, jump over and remove the hurdles from your path and keep moving forward. Don't allow stress and depression to slow you down or stop you.

-If you spend too much time staying depressed, happiness will remain an illusion. No matter what stresses you, try to make yourself happy under any circumstance. Always be aware that the time we had to live on this planet is very short.

-No matter how much pain and suffering you have been through and are still coming through, know that you deserve better and can get better. Never become too depressed. It will make you hopeless and make you make worse choices out of desperation. This is how I talk to myself. Sorry if I was too loud

-No matter what situation we find ourselves in, we have to either learn how to survive, or we will just allow difficulties to worsen our reality.

- When you feel stressed, angry, or depressed, find a way to de-stress and calm yourself down right away. Don't stay stressed and angry. And do not resort to alcohol and drug to do that. Not the solution.

WORDS OF INSPIRATION

-Use your mind to calm your mind down. You have the mental strength to mentally deal with stress and anger. If you don't, you will drive yourself insane.

-Don't make assumptions about people's reality based on what you see. You have no idea how much pain, suffering, and unhappiness they are silently going through.

- People can look happy but be going through a whole lot and not showing it.

-Everybody has some type of unhappy or stressful situation they dealing with that you might have no idea about. So try to understand people instead of judging them. Let's be compassionate and kind to one another.

-Don't worry about yourself too much when everything is not going your way. You are still alive, therefore able to try to make things a little better.

-Take it easy on your mind.

-Please, be happy or try to make yourself happy no matter what you are going through.

- Without happiness and peacefulness, life is not enjoyable no matter how much money and possession you have.

- Find something in your life to be happy about.

- I am walking by the cemetery to just reflect on life and my purpose in being here and whether I am using my time on this earth consciously, to make a positive contribution to humanity before my time is up and I am laid to rest in a place like this.

-Death is not what I am afraid of. I only hope that I can accomplish my purpose here before I make that transition and that when I am gone, humanity can remember me for something good. No matter what is going on in our life, we can still make a difference to make life better on Earth.

- I am admiring the beauty in my surroundings. Sometimes, the mind can be so consumed by worries that we pay little to no attention to the natural as well as man-created beauty in the surroundings that we are navigating through. Please, stop worrying too much about everything or little things. Just look around and you will see a lot of beautiful things to take your mind to another dimension where life can be contemplated for the beauty in it.

-One thing I have learned about stress is that it keeps you busy worrying. Worrying too much is exhausting, mentally and physically. If you are so busy worrying, it will wear you out and make you feel unable to make moves because your energy will be so low. So please, take a break from worrying. Take actions to make things better, no matter what is distressing you. Leo

-I went through so much hell for so long that I learned to keep my sanity by finding a way to create happiness within and sometimes around me.

- Those who followed my page since last spring can see how I made living in a tent under trees and in bushes, pleasant. So, I am not here to tell you to not be real with how you feel when the reality within and outside of you is painful and disturbing or just hard. All I am saying is that you still have to deal with it either by just allowing your predicament of undesirable circumstances to make you miserable and depressed or just sad, or just by enduring and find something to be happy about.

When you walk down the street feeling sad and worrying, please take your mind off your worries for just a minute and observe your surroundings. Lift your head up, and you might notice beautiful clouds. Or just pay attention to the buildings in your sight, and you may love their beautiful architectural designs. Or just observe the plants and trees or even the bugs and you will beauty and wonders around you.

-Life is happening around you whether you feel hopeless or not. So, be hopeful and try and try and try and try, and never despair or give up trying. There is always an end to a tunnel. Keep trying to get to it.

I-I am About to get up and start my day. Though I live outside, I am grateful to be able to wake up today and look at this beautiful nature around me and breathe the fresh and unpolluted air. I am grateful.

Everything is not that bad. We are surrounded by beauty from nature and also from human creativity and artistry.

There is so much to be grateful for no matter the predicament we in. Don't let stress suck the energy out of you. It is a beautiful day out there. Let me get up and take advantage of a bright sunny day.

It is raining outside. I am in here working on my next. Always occupy yourself constructively, even on a rainy day, whether you are homeless or you live a normal life. Don't make time for stress and depression to occupy your time.

Just woke up in my tent and observing the sun rising. Always a blessing to wake up to experience another day. When you wake up to see another day, don't stress about your problems. Instead, just be grateful and make the best of the day.

Leo Gnawa (Source Instagram/homelesslivesmatterbook)

CHAPTER 21

HOMELESSNESS IS NOT A CHOICE

"Hi Leo, I don't know if you remember me but I'm the Australian who bought a copy of your book from you in early January. I wanted to let you know that I just finished reading it and it was really quiet eye opening. Even on the other side of the world it's clear there's room for many of your experiences, thoughts, and ideas to be applied here too. Thanks for painting this issue in a new light for me, I will strive to be more compassionate and a bigger advocate for homeless rights than I was before. Billy". Messages like this one that I received on March 13, 2023, from Billy in Australia, humble me and make me commit more to my work.

I feel like society has become more apathetic towards the homeless and poor people in general. There are more and more homeless individuals and their tents visible on the streets, and society seems to have accepted it as normal. There is no public outrage about it. I think we should try to help and support and be more compassionate and not always try to condemn others for their predicament.

HOMELESS PEOPLE ARE HUMAN BEINGS TOO

I rushed to the metro station at Rhode Island Avenue to get on the next train to Silver Spring, on my way home. It was 7:26pm. I was about to tap my card to the gate to get in. At the same time, my attention was drawn by a gentleman who was very upset. He looked like he was in his late 20's or early 30's. He had Puerto Rican or Dominican features. He kept looking around on the floor and walked half-way towards the station entrance and turned back around. He asked the attendant if he had seen a phone that he said he lost. He described it. The attendant answer was negative. He entered the station after me. He approached me as I was about to get on the escalator and asked me if he could use my phone to call his sister. He told me that she had just bought him the phone the same day. He did not memorize the phone number, so he wanted her to call his phone to see if she could locate it.

I know what it feels like to lose a phone. I myself had lost my phone on the train a month earlier. I exited the train but realized that I did not have my phone on me when I went downstairs to exit the station. The train had left by then and was heading towards the next station on the way to Glenmont Station, its final destination about 4 stations away. The attendant asked me to get back on the platform upstairs and wait for the train to return back in the next five minutes. I tried to remember which car I should get in and check, when the train came back in the opposite direction. But I thought it was a waste of time, since I could not remember exactly which car I was in. The train had 6 cars. But I was fortunate enough because a lady passenger found it. I went to purchase another phone the next day and was able to get in touch with her and get my phone back. I gave her $40.

I normally feel apprehensive about letting a stranger use my phone in a public place, but I felt sorry for him.

I handed him my phone and stood close enough. He called his sister, but the call went straight into the answering service. He tried to call again a couple of times, but he was out of luck. He left a message on the answering service. He then handed me my phone back and thanked me. But I heard him say something about going to the shelter, when he was leaving a message on her answering service. I asked him where he was staying. He answered that he was staying at a shelter in Rockville. He thanked me again and headed to the escalator. I called him back and handed him the money I had on me. It was not much. Maybe $8 or $9. "That's for me?" He said. " Yes. I used to be homeless for over ten years. So, we together man " I added. When I got to the top on the platform, he told me" look, I need to tell you this. You gave me this money, but I feel bad because I am an addict and I will most likely get high with it, although I already have some stuff on me". He did not tell me what he was addicted to and what he had on him, but I assumed that he was talking about crack cocaine. I know a lot of people are conflicted whether to give or not to a homeless begging them for money, because they assume that the homeless person may use the money for alcohol or drug instead of food. I think that unless you know for certain that the money you give will be misused, you should not make assumptions about what a person is going to do with it. Now, if a person comes to you and tells you that he needs some money to get a drink or get high, or if you know for sure that he or she will use your money to get drunk or high, then you will make your decision to give to them or not, based on the facts and not on assumption.

I answered" look, you are fine, don't feel bad, I am not here to judge you. I just hope that one day, you get some help with your addiction. But don't feel bad. I gave it to you, and it is yours." I wanted him to keep the money, because he was honest enough to tell me that he had an addiction problem after I gave him the $8 or $9. Sometimes we don't know why people get addicted to alcohol or drugs. This is why I prefer to show compassion and help the best I can, instead of condemning a person who is sick. All I can do is comfort and encourage him to seek help.

HOMELESSNESS IS NOT A CHOICE AND ENDING IT IS NOT EASY

I was watching a video on the YouTube channel of a vlogger from outside the US, who was visiting Washington DC. She was shocked to see so many homeless people on the streets. She made a video about it near the homeless camp that was in McPherson Square, the park on 15th and K Streets in downtown Washington. In the video, she said that she was told by her friends who reside in the Washington DC area, that most of the homeless choose to be homeless and refuse to be housed or to work. I wish I had met her and given her my book Homeless Lives Matter, Homeless My Story, so that she could know that most of what she was told are stereotypes that I dispelled in the book. But let's me say this. I disagree with folks who claim that most people who are homeless choose to be homeless.

To think that all homeless people are either drug addicts, mentally ill or unwilling to work and therefore making a conscious choice to be homeless, is not the right way to understand homelessness.

The problem with people who don't want to feel sorry for the homeless and only want to blame them for what they are going through, is that they only think of homeless people as drug addicts, mentally ill and lazy people, who prefer to leave outside than go to work.

HOMELESS PEOPLE ARE HUMAN BEINGS TOO

It is a fact that, a great number of homeless visible on the streets of major US cities including Washington DC are the mentally ill, drug or alcohol addicts and unemployed ones. But truth of the matter is that there are more homeless men and women and young folks who are not mentally ill, drug addicts or unemployed. They are not the ones who people see every day on the street corner. They are the invisible homeless. They dress nicely, look clean and blend in with normal people. You ride the bus or the subway with them every day or sit at coffee shops next to them while they are working on their laptop, but you have no idea that they are homeless. They go to work every day, and their co-workers don't even know that they are homeless. Unfortunately, the stereotypical idea of a homeless person is the mentally ill, the drug addict, the unemployed who hangs in parks or sleep outside. But many homeless sleep in their cars, on a friend's couch or even in the tents downtown. They sneak in them at night without anybody noticing.

To say that they are homeless because they are lazy and don't want to work is incorrect and unfair. Many homeless folks do have a job or go to work every day. But they are not earning enough to afford rent, in a city where cost of living is high and living wage is higher than minimum wage. That means that a lot of homeless who earn minimum wage cannot afford cost of living here in Washington DC. So having a job is not necessarily a remedy for homelessness, if the job is not paying enough to afford cost of living in this expensive city.

You will agree that the majority of your relatives, friends, neighbors, co-workers who are unemployed, alcoholics, drug and substance addicts or mentally ill, are not homeless.

I don't think that homeless people who have issues with drug or alcohol addiction, mental illness, unemployment, and some other issues, deserve to be homeless. Until you know why they are on the street and what they went through in life, do not judge the homeless, that you see out there struggling with addiction, mental illness, unemployment, and other issues prevalent in the homeless communities.

CHAPTER 21

MESSAGE FROM A HOMELESS MAN TO YOUNG PEOPLE SO THEY WON'T BE HOMELESS

One day

I was in my tent worrying too much

Life whispered this into my mind

Homeless man

Stop worrying yourself

Understand your reality

Make intelligent decisions

Be logical, be open-minded

Seek guidance on how to deal with life better

Never try to give up

And never give up trying

You will make progress

and be successful

Have goals and a purpose

And seek to accomplish them

while you still can

I listened and tried my best

And things got better and better

Until I figured a way out of homelessness

Hard life taught me that I have to have a purpose in life, otherwise, the life I live is just survival and struggle with no real happiness but only stress.

Many times, when I walked by a cemetery, mostly at night, I stepped closer to the fence and spent few minutes there to meditate and reflect about the fact that I am here in this human reality for a brief time, and that I will also die sooner or later. What I am afraid of is to die without having accomplished anything meaningful with y life. As I am aging (I am 59-year-old now, 2024), I realize that time is going so fast, and I don't have much time left. There are things in life that if you do not do now, it will be too late later.

If you are a young person, finish your education instead of keep dropping out of school and keep hoping that you have enough time to go back and finish your education later. One of the things that I regret the most in my life is that I never finished my education. I dropped out of my second year of college. I would have loved to have had a couple of PhDs by now. But it is ok. I am still happy to have written books, motivated and reached thousands of people.

If I die today, my books will survive me. Hundreds of years from now, my books will still be here and keep me alive in the memory of generations to come. I am therefore satisfied somehow that I still was able to accomplish something that will survive me, although I did it later than sooner because of all the difficulties I went through.

I see a lot of young people who are homeless. Some of them are teenagers. I wonder, why aren't they in school? If you are a young man or lady who is not working and not in school, please do something with your life. Don't just be content about living day to day with no purpose.

You are wasting your precious life if you idle all day and every day with bad company and engage in unproductive activities that will land you into chronic homelessness, in poverty or in trouble with the law.

You have to have a purpose and some goals that you need to accomplish to give some meaning to your life.

You must value time because there is so much that you can accomplish, if you take your life seriously and do not fool around and waste your time doing nothing productive.

When you are young, you think that you have too much time ahead of you to do what you want. That is true to a certain degree. But it is also true that time is shorter than you realize. What we call time is nothing but the movement of the earth around the sun. Once the earth goes around the sun one time, which is called a revolution and happens every 365 days six hours and 9 minutes, we call it a year. When the earth turns around itself or its axis to be exact, it's called a rotation. When it happens every 23 hours and 56 minutes (rounded to 24 hours), we call it a day.

Whether we do what we have to do or not, the earth is not going to stop moving around the sun and wait for us to do what we need to do. Your body will tell you when your time gets shorter. You will not be able to run, jump and move as fast as you could years earlier, when you get older.

When you age, you will not be as strong as you are now. There are things you can do today that you cannot do later. While you still have time, try to accomplish something great with your life.

If you want to live a successful and fulfilling life, you need to have a purpose and do what you need to do to achieve your purpose. Simple as that. I told myself that, while I was homeless, living in a tent or sleeping on somebody's couch for decades.

MESSAGE FROM A HOMELESS MAN TO YOUNG PEOPLE

You need to learn how to survive and take care of your basic needs, if you want to live a normal life and not end up homeless or poor as I did for a long time. If you are having difficulties surviving in this world that is becoming more and more complicated, then your life is going to be very hard, miserable, and depressing.

Animals can survive by using their natural instinct to seek food and protect and defend themselves from danger. But most animals are not just surviving. They are playing a role in the ecosystem by interacting with the environment to make life sustainable on this planet.

Life is possible on earth because every single being, from the invisible microbes to the immense planets and stars far above us, is playing an essential role in life on earth.

If the tiny bees decided to survive with no purpose as some of us human beings do, then 180,000 plant species will not be fertilized, because pollen will not move from one flower to another on their own.

We cannot just reduce our existence to feeding, clothing, sheltering and entertaining ourselves, and gratifying our desires.

Unlike other species in the animal kingdom, you and I, humans are endowed with greater potentials, greater intelligence, and a creative spirit that supersede our reliance on instinct alone for survival.

You and I may not achieve the same greatness as the heroes and venerated individuals whose names are given to buildings, schools, bridges, institutions, towns, cities, countries, rivers, and lakes because of their exceptional contribution to society and life in general. But we can find our purpose on this earth and live a productive and fulfilling life and contribute to the betterment of humanity. Or we can at least, leave a good memory of us after we are dead and gone. Otherwise, our existence will be less meaningful than that of animals trying to survive in the wilderness.

Whoever created you and I gave us a powerful brain that no other existing beings possess. Let us use it to think hard about the meaning of our existence on this earth and what our purpose must be.

Don't just live life day after day and just worry about what you going to eat the next hour, where you are going to sleep tonight, what music you are going to listen or dance to all day, and who you are going to have fun with. There is more to your existence on earth than your day-to-day survival. You are here for a purpose, just like the bees, the ants, and every other creature. Find your purpose and your survival will be meaningful.

It was a time when I felt like my life was doomed. I felt like I was living from one day to the next day and was surviving and not living to achieve any purpose. And I was not happy living like that.

If that is your experience with life, tell yourself as I did, "I cannot live to just survive. I must find my purpose on earth and be happy while contributing to make the world a better place and leave a positive impact long after I am gone."

.

I heard the man say something about the homeless guy who sells his book around here. He was a middle-aged white professional-looking well-dressed man. He was leaving the restaurant at Old Ebbitt Grill and stopped in front of a guy shining shoes in the front outside. "I bought a book from a homeless writer outside here the last time I was here. Have you seen him today? I heard him, although I was about 30 feet away. I got up immediately and walked straight to him through the sizable crowd of folks hanging out for a cigarette break or going in and out of Old Ebbitt Grill. He had his back turned towards me. The shoeshine guy pointed at me, "You talking about him?" "I am so happy to see you. Your book changed my life. I used to not care about the homeless until I read your book. It changed me. Now, I am committed to helping the homeless" said the man to me.

It made me happy to hear that I was able to create awareness about homeless and motivate a reader of my works to become involved with doing something to help the homeless. To me, happiness is the ultimate goal of my existence.

If you struggle every day to survive but you are not happy with your life, then what is success worth? We all long to be happy, otherwise, even a successful life is meaningless if you still feel unhappy despite your accomplishments. But how can you even be happy if your life is a daily struggle, and if you can barely feed yourself and meet your basic needs? I couldn't. I had to do something that I care about, and which gives me not just inner gratification but also allows me to become self-sufficient and socially stable.

The day I decided that I needed to have a clear purpose and strive to achieve it, is when I committed to not be content with being without and with relying on charity to survive. The state of mind of not having a clear purpose in life but just worrying about food, clothes, and shelter daily, got me stuck in the predicament I was in and clouded my ability to see a better situation ahead for myself. I ended up remaining in chronic homelessness for a long time and learned how to adjust to it. It became a normal way of life for me. If you are dealing with a bad situation that has lasted so long and have become adjusted to it, you have to convince yourself that you can overcome your dilemma and live a better life and be happy in this world. But you have to define a clear purpose for your life and define clear goals to achieve, to make progress from the bad place you are in to a better place you need to be.

Thinking like that motivated me to come up with a serious plan to remove myself from homelessness and achieve something with my life that will make me Self-sufficient and prosperous. Like I said, I was homeless. But since, February 2021 to be exact, I am no longer homeless. I decided that I would give my life a purpose and come up with a plan to make it happen.

So, the question to me was, what shall I do to remove myself permanently. from chronic homelessness and be in a better situation to achieve my purpose in life. What would that purpose in life be?

In 2009, when I was selling my copies of Street Sense (the Washington DC homeless newspaper) in front of the Metro Station at Dupont Circle and the Wholefoods store on 14th street, in Northwest Washington DC, I had few regular customers who used to tell me that I was a great writer. Also, from time to time, I would go to the park in Dupont Circle and walk around and try to sell my copies of Street Sense to the folks resting in the park. I sat by a Catholic priest who had read my article in a previous edition. He looked at me in the eyes and told me, you are a very good writer. I looked at him and said, "Not really". Then he admonished me for not believing in myself being a good writer.

So, when I sat in my tent that day in 2016 and told myself that I had enough grey matter in my brain to figure a way out of my misery, that is when I purposed myself to achieve something greater than worrying about my life and getting nowhere but getting stressed out and depressed.

Most of the time, we prolong our predicament because we fail to realize that we have within us, the talents and gift or ability to solve our problems. I decided to use my love for writing as a tool to achieve my purpose. To me, a purpose is an ultimate ideal that we want to reach in life to feel fulfilled and become successful. The purpose is like the final destination of a traveler on a long journey. My purpose is to contribute to the upliftment of my fellow human beings, and the betterment of humanity, through activism, writing, and other actions.

You cannot and should not just live life without any purpose and just survive with no ambition or desire for a better life. You have to have a dream of an ideal reality and try to materialize it.

Whatever goals or purpose you have in life, you must plant the seeds in fertile soil and water them. You will see your plans materialize slowly but surely. You can stay on your knees all your life and pray or wish for good luck to change your predicament, but waiting on a miracle without taking any action to make things better can disable you and prolong your condition. There is so much you can do for yourself if you don't believe in yourself.

You can try your best to figure out a way out of your predicament, or you can just sit there, get stuck and let things get worse. It is your choice to do something about what you are going through or just give up on yourself and make your life worse. You cannot get anything accomplished if you don't believe that you can. You have to believe in yourself and try hard to make it happen.

Animals get up as soon as the sun rises and get busy doing what they have to do to feed and take care of themselves, in an hostile and dangerous environment where they are constantly being preyed on by other animals. One day, I was in my tent, sleeping. I opened my eyes and saw a hawk fly low and snatch a small bird that was trying to find something to eat in front of my tent.

If you are lazy and want everything free in life and do not want to make any effort to make things better for yourself, you can pray all you want, nothing is going to happen. You cannot just be frustrated about life or your condition and just stay depressed and pray for God to come and do for you what you can do for yourself and expect an answer to your prayer.

You have to believe in yourself because whoever created you equipped you with the tools to deal with difficulties just like they did with other living beings.

To believe in yourself means to have confidence in yourself and not feel defeated and hopeless or insecure about your ability to resolve difficult issues you are facing. To believe in yourself is being able to say yes, I can. Yes, I can do my very best to make my life better and deal with my issues better. To talk to yourself like that, is a great attitude that will encourage you to do what needs to be done.

Things may be difficult, but make a way for yourself and make it easy on yourself. Always believe that you can make it easier and better.

Be courageous in life if you want to make it. Don't just give up because things are tough. You are going to fail if you do not arm yourself with courage and face adversity. Things are not going to be as easy as you expected. But you have to go through the process and figure a way to jump over or go around the hurdles on your path and keep going ahead. You can't just say, oh no, this is too much, I am not going through this. Things are not just going to happen for you. You have to make it happen.

You have to be persistent. You can't just start something and put it on hold, and start it back, and put it on hold, and wonder why things are not happening as fast as you desire.

It was a time when I did not have a bike because the bike I had was stolen. I had to either walk from my tent to wherever. When I could, I would catch a bus from downtown to my tent late at night. Other times, I kept walking until I got to my tent. It was a 40-minute walk. At times, I was so tired but so sleepy. I wanted to get to my tent as soon as possible, but my body wanted to stop and rest for a minute and my eyes were about to close. But I used to keep telling myself, "the faster you walk, the closer you get".

"Leo, keep moving. The faster you walk the closer you get, "I kept saying that to myself, until I got to my tent and jumped on my bed and went to sleep. I understand that sometimes you are tired and want to pause for a minute. But you are delaying your progress when you stop too often.

You have to be consistent. You can't just start something and then switch up to something else as soon, as you realize that the path towards achieving what you started is not going to be as easy as you thought. Unless you realize that what you wanted to accomplish was unrealistic and unachievable as you planned it in the first place, stay the course until you make it.

Don't let other people discourage you or make you doubt yourself. Be courageous and persistent.

I sold my books on the street, under extreme cold weather for hours many times. My fingers and toes were frozen, but I had to endure. I means that I had to force myself to stay outside on the street and sell my book despite the suffering that I went through. People seeing me staying in the cold instead of packing and leaving, had more empathy for me and went ahead and bought a copy of my book because they admired my resiliency. Be willing to make sacrifices. Don't expect things to happen that easily for you. Everything is not going to be comfortable or convenient. But you have to endure till you succeed. Believe in yourself.

CONCLUSION:

MYTHS & FACTS ABOUT HOMELESSNESS

(Source: https://www.councilforthehomeless.org/myths-facts-about-homelessness/)

<u>Myth: People who are homeless should just get a job and then they would not be homeless.</u>

Fact: Many people who are homeless do have jobs... The National Coalition for the Homeless estimates as many as 40%-60% of people experiencing homelessness nationwide are employed. However, a paycheck does not necessarily solve their homelessness or other challenges.

<u>Myth: People choose to be homeless.</u>

Fact: This myth is dangerous and allows us to ignore the trauma of homelessness and neurobiological effects trauma has on humans. Being homeless is stressful, humiliating, exhausting, and dangerous. It is a hard day-to-day existence for men, women, and children.... Homelessness is traumatic and complicated, and solutions are not a one-size-fits-all.

Myth: People who are homeless are dangerous, violent, and/or criminals.

CONCLUSION

Fact: A person who is homeless is no more likely to be a criminal than a person who is housed, with one legal exception: camping ordinances. People who are homeless break that law merely by being unhoused. The reality is that most spend their time and resources trying to survive and improve their situation.

Rather than being dangerous or lawbreakers, they are parents trying to work or find a job while they live in a car with their children. They are teens who have no supportive adults in their lives while they try to find a place to live, so they can hopefully stay in school. They are senior citizens with poor health and a fixed income struggling to get by. People who are homeless are more likely to be victims of a crime than to commit a crime.

<u>Myth: Housing should come with conditions like being clean and sober.</u>

Fact: Evidence tells us that people who are homeless can find stability and healing when provided empowering supports focused on housing and supports. Known as Housing First, this approach acknowledges the complexities of addiction, trauma, and the challenges that come with experiencing homelessness. It also acknowledges that it can be very difficult to successfully address challenges while living on the streets or in an unsafe and unstable situation.

WHY DO PEOPLE EXPERIENCE HOMELESSNESS?

Here are the reason why people are homeless according to the National Coalition for the Homeless, a Washington DC based homeless advocacy group:

Housing

There are currently two major contributors to the housing and homelessness crises: a lack of low cost housing nationwide and the limited scale of housing assistance programs.

Nationally, the cost of rental housing greatly exceeds wages earned by low-income renter households. For example, a full-time worker needs to earn on average $25.82 per hour to afford a modest two-bedroom rental and $21.21 hourly to afford a one-bedroom (National Low Income Housing Coalition, 2022). However, the national minimum wage is only $7.25!

Housing isn't only out of reach for minimum wage earners. The 2022 housing wage is far higher than the median hourly rate earned by customer service workers ($17.75), nursing assistants ($14.57), maintenance and repair workers ($20.76), home health aides ($14.15), retail workers ($14.03), and many others in the workforce.

CONCLUSION

Poverty

Homelessness and poverty are inextricably linked. Poor people are frequently unable to pay for housing, food, childcare, health care, and education. Difficult choices must be made when limited resources cover only some of these necessities. Often it is housing, which absorbs a high proportion of income that must be dropped. If you are poor, you are essentially an illness, an accident, or a paycheck away from living on the streets.

According to the United States Census Bureau, the national poverty rate in 2016 was 12.7%. There were 40.6 million people in poverty. While the poverty rate has been slowly declining since 2014, a couple of factors account for continuing poverty:

Lack of Employment Opportunities – With unemployment rates remaining high, jobs are hard to find in the current economy. Even if people can find work, this does not automatically provide an escape from poverty.

Decline in Available Public Assistance – The declining value and availability of public assistance is another source of increasing poverty and homelessness and many families leaving welfare struggle to get medical care, food, and housing as a result of loss of benefits, low wages, and unstable employment. Additionally, most states have not replaced the old welfare system with an alternative that enables families and individuals to obtain above-poverty employment and to sustain themselves when work is not available or possible.

Other major factors, which can contribute to homelessness, include:

Lack of Affordable Health Care – For families and individuals struggling to pay the rent, a serious illness or disability can start a downward spiral into homelessness, beginning with a lost job, depletion of savings to pay for care, and eventual eviction.

Domestic Violence – Battered women who live in poverty are often forced to choose between abusive relationships and homelessness. In addition, 50% of the cities surveyed by the U.S. Conference of Mayors identified domestic violence as a primary cause of homelessness (U.S. Conference of Mayors, 2005).

Mental Illness – Approximately 16% of the single adult homeless population suffers from some form of severe and persistent mental illness (U.S. Conference of Mayors, 2005).

Addiction – The relationship between addiction and homelessness is complex and controversial. Many people who are addicted to alcohol and drugs never become homeless, but

CONCLUSION

people who are poor and addicted are clearly at increased risk of homelessness.

Made in the USA
Middletown, DE
27 November 2024

65580162R00090